SIGNS &
SYMBOLS

First published in Great Britain in 2025 by Godsfield, an imprint of
Octopus Publishing Group Ltd
Carmelite House
50 Victoria Embankment
London EC4Y 0DZ
www.octopusbooks.co.uk

An Hachette UK Company
www.hachette.co.uk

The authorized representative in the EEA is Hachette Ireland,
8 Castlecourt Centre, Dublin 15, D15 XTP3, Ireland (email: info@hbgi.ie)

Some of this material previously appeared in *The Signs and Symbols Bible*.

Distributed in the US by Hachette Book Group
1290 Avenue of the Americas, 4th and 5th Floors
New York, NY 10104

Distributed in Canada by Canadian Manda Group
664 Annette St., Toronto, Ontario, Canada M6S 2C8

ISBN 97-8-184181-640-1

A CIP catalogue record for this book is available from the British Library.

Printed and bound in China.

10 9 8 7 6 5 4 3 2 1

Publisher: Lucy Pessell
Designer: Isobel Platt
Senior Editor: Tim Leng
Assistant Editor: Samina Rahman
Production Controller: Allison Gonsalves

Images: iStock

Madonna Gauding

SIGNS & SYMBOLS

AN ENCYCLOPEDIA OF ORIGINS & SACRED CONCEPTS

GODSFIELD

CONTENTS

1

INTRODUCTION

A symbol is something that stands for, or represents, something other than what it is. The word 'symbol' is based on the Greek verb *symballein*, meaning 'to toss together' or 'to join together'. *Symballein* also suggests a hiding or veiling of meaning.

Symbols, signs and glyphs

Symbol-making has been a deep-seated trait of humans since at least the times of the hunter-gatherers. To give an example, consider the image of an animal – a lion. The lion may be understood as the King of the Jungle and in that role it may be associated with courage, fearlessness, strength, royalty and power. The lion is now no longer just an animal, but a symbol of many human qualities.

If it appears on a family crest, the lion may symbolize that family and its ancestors going back in time. The lion may also symbolize a king and his entire dominion. 'Lion' was the nickname given to medieval rulers who had a reputation for bravery, such as Richard I of England, who was also known as Richard the Lionheart. And as guardian figures placed outside a palace, a pair of lion statues may represent superior military prowess and communicate that unlawful entry will be met with devastating attack.

As you can see, the simple image of a lion has over time become a series of ideas joined together, and the lion plus its many associations is now a symbol. Given the length of time that humans have coexisted with lions, this animal has both ancient archetypal associations and symbolic meanings that are tied to specific contexts and cultures.

DECODING THE DIVINE

So, it is clear that humans make symbols in order to communicate ideas. But we also make symbols to help communicate and understand higher truths that are veiled or hidden to ordinary consciousness.

The Greek gods – each with their distinctive form and personality – were not anthropomorphic (that is, having human characteristics), but rather were symbols of a single divine being whose true nature is not personal or even comprehensible by humans. The gods functioned as symbols of qualities of the divine filtered through a human lens.

The same can be said of Buddhist deities. Tara and Yamantaka are unique figures in the Buddhist pantheon: one male, one female, each with his or her hand implements and number of arms and heads, in an active or resting posture. Yet both represent aspects of one enlightened mind as it manifests in infinite ways.

The signs and symbols associated with the image of the Buddha communicate aspects of his enlightened nature. Those who are knowledgeable about these symbols and their meanings can look at this image and acquire a deeper insight into the human potential for enlightenment. And when Christ wears a crown, as Christ the King, Christians understand that his dominion over all creatures is an essential part of his nature and not acquired by violence; his crown does not symbolize human power, but rather the act of loving and serving others. Symbols speak in layers of meaning and provide a shorthand for different ideas. Divine figures and images are human attempts to symbolize the ineffable – that which cannot be expressed in words. They also present the surface of that which is hidden and veiled, which may require deeper exploration.

POINTING THE WAY

Whereas a symbol always stands for something more than its immediate meaning and challenges us to go beyond the surface, to discover rich, expansive layers of significance, a sign points the way. A lion may symbolize many ideas and qualities that cannot necessarily be put into words, whereas an image of a lion (together with an arrow) at the zoo probably points the way to the lion cages – and is a sign. Some things, such as a wedding ring, can function as both sign and symbol. A ring is a sign that the person wearing it is married and it is a symbol of any number of ideas, such as fidelity, love, romance and devotion. Its circular shape symbolizes eternal love with no beginning and no end.

Glyphs are picture symbols that represent an object or concept, and they fall somewhere between a sign and a symbol. They differ from symbols in that they are usually more graphic and less prone to varying interpretations, yet they communicate more meaning than signs. In contemporary culture, a crossed red circle superimposed on a picture of a dog is a glyph representing the simple idea that dogs (and perhaps other pets) are not welcome. Whole early written languages, such as Egyptian hieroglyphs, were based on glyphs or pictograms.

Archetypes

Carl Jung (1875–1961), the Swiss psychiatrist and founder of analytical psychology, believed that looking at symbol creation would provide a key to understanding human nature. A symbol, as defined by Jung, is the best possible expression of something that is essentially difficult to explain or know. Investigating the symbols of religious, mythological and magical systems from many cultures and time periods, he discovered remarkable similarities. To account for these, Jung suggested that the unconscious is divided into two layers. The first layer of the unconscious, which he called the *personal unconscious*, is the reservoir of material acquired by an individual through their life that they have mostly forgotten or repressed.

The second layer of the unconscious, which Jung named the *collective unconscious*, contains the cellular memories that are common to all of humankind. These common memories and experiences form archetypes – or primordial, symbolic images that reflect basic patterns and universal themes that are common to all peoples.

UNIVERSAL ARCHETYPES

Archetypes exist outside of space and time. Examples of archetypes identified by Jung are the Shadow, the Old Wise Person, the Anima, the Animus, the Trickster, the Mother, the Father and the Innocent Child. There are also many nature archetypes that are common to all people, such as fire, ocean, river, mountain, sky and tree. Gods and goddesses and the heroes and heroines of world myths also function as archetypes.

Jung discovered that, because of the collective unconscious, humans have a disposition to react to life in the same way as the human beings who have gone before. He discovered patterns which are distinctly human that structure our minds and imaginations. This pattern is realized when an image from the collective unconscious enters the consciousness of a person in some way, such as through dreams or myths. For example, the Old Wise Person may appear in the dreams of three different people, featuring as a loving grandmother in Kansas in one dream, as a tramp on the street in London in another and as an old woman healer in Africa in a third. Despite the differences, for each person the dream still refers back to the archetype of the Old Wise Person. Archetypes and archetypal images also appear in novels, films, music and plays.

Jung postulated that, as human beings, we share in a single universal unconscious, the *collective unconscious*. And he believed that even the first layer of the unconscious, the personal unconscious, is shaped according to patterns that are universal. Learning about symbols helps us to have greater awareness and power in our own lives.

Because of inborn ways of perceiving the world, and our shared unconscious material, many of the symbols that are collected in this book may have a powerful influence on us without us necessarily even thinking consciously about them. Advertisers, for instance, use archetypal symbols to great effect in selling their products. A good example is the Marlboro Man, a Wild Man symbol in the form of the American cowboy. The Leo Burnett advertising agency created this hyper-masculine figure to sell filtered cigarettes to GIs returning from the Second World War, who were used to smoking unfiltered cigarettes and thought of filtered cigarettes as effeminate.

HIDDEN KNOWLEDGE

As Jung has so eloquently proved, symbols are not only the language of the unconscious, but also of the occult. The word 'occult' comes from the Latin *occultus*, meaning 'hidden' and therefore refers to 'knowledge of the hidden'.

In the English language this means 'knowledge of the paranormal', as opposed to knowledge obtained as a result of science. The occult relates to the study of a deeper spiritual reality that extends beyond pure reason and the physical sciences. The term is also used as a label that is given to a number of mystical organizations or orders, such as the alchemists and those who practised ceremonial witchcraft, and to the teachings and practices as taught by them. The name also extends to a large body of literature and spiritual philosophy.

Many of the symbols in this book refer to hidden spiritual knowledge, both Eastern and Western. In later life Jung added to his theories by suggesting that the deepest levels of the unconscious touched on the paranormal and lay outside the bounds of time, space and causality. This level was both of and beyond universal consciousness. It was this deeper level that held the promise of spiritual realization and the possibility of enlightenment.

About this book

There is never unanimity over the meaning and representation of symbols, but the descriptions in this book reflect the most commonly held interpretations. Some symbols are ancient and have changed form over time; different versions of them may exist. But the differences do not take away from their archetypal power.

The world of symbols is dynamic and changes as knowledge and customs change. Yet symbols retain aspects of universal wisdom and meaning to which humans have responded throughout time, and continue to respond. As you will discover in the following pages, the history of symbolism shows that everything around us can assume symbolic significance:

• Natural objects (such as stones, plants, animals, mountains, valleys, the sun and the moon)
• Human-made things (such as temples, houses, tools, ritual items and calendars)
• Abstract forms (such as shapes, colours and numbers).

Everything in the cosmos becomes a potential symbol, because humans unconsciously transform objects or images into symbols and thereby endow them with great psychological or religious importance. The confluence of religion and art, reaching back into prehistoric times, has left a record of those symbols that were meaningful to our ancestors.

This book collects symbols from ancient civilizations (pages 18–41), from Western and Middle Eastern religions (pages 42– 55) and from the Eastern religions. It covers secular and religious symbols of power, of heraldry and of alchemy, astrology and ceremonial magic. It describes the symbols of the natural world: animals, plants and minerals, crystals and gemstones. It also collects amulet and talisman symbols, letter symbols and symbols relating to time, shape, number and colour.

READING THE SYMBOLS

Wherever you are, you are wrapped in symbols. This book will increase your awareness of symbols as they appear in your everyday life, opening you to an intense experience of meaning as you travel throughout your day. All forms of art (including music, architecture, sculpture and painting) and all forms of literature and moving images (including novels, plays, poetry, films and television shows) are filled with symbolic meaning. Many advertisements (both print and digital) use symbolism in subtle ways. Viewing them with a critical eye can be interesting and enlightening. So use this book to learn about the symbols that you will now begin to see all around you.

Paying attention to your dreams, and writing them down every morning, will give you insight into what the archetypal images are trying to tell you. Dream symbols can be powerfully transformative if you make the effort to become conscious of them and work with them.

When visiting a museum or art gallery, take this book along for reference. The artist may or may not have been conscious of the symbols that appear in his or her work. If interesting objects or figures emerge, explore their symbolic meaning to enhance your experience. If you are viewing ancient or medieval art, the symbols will usually be found in this book.

Once you have read this book, you will notice how various symbols are used every time you see a film or read a novel. In your daily life you will be able to work with symbols to consciously embody the energies and meanings that are important to you. When deciding what sort of flowers to send to a friend, for example, you can select those that symbolize the deeper meaning you wish to communicate. You can choose to wear a particular gemstone for its special healing and energetic qualities and for what it stands for in your life. When decorating your home, you can select art objects, paintings and furnishings that include the symbols with which you would like to surround yourself. If you choose a statue of the Buddha, you will be able to understand the spiritual meaning symbolized by its various aspects.

You can read this book through from cover to cover or simply keep it for reference, looking up symbols as you go. Either way, the following chapters are your key to the secret, potent, healing world of symbols.

2

SYMBOLS
DIRECTORY

ANCIENT CIVILIZATIONS

Some symbols can be traced back to ancient civilizations when humans used them both to communicate and to represent the world in which they lived and died. They developed systems to study the sun, moon and stars, and sophisticated cosmologies to explain the origin of the universe. Living in a world that was mysterious and unpredictable, they identified a pantheon of archetypal gods and goddesses. From them they sought both protection and blessings, and through them accessed the ineffable – those divine truths and realizations beyond the limitations of the ordinary human mind.

The Egyptians

The unification of Upper and Lower Egypt, in around 3200 BCE, gave rise to dynastic Egypt, one of the oldest civilizations in the world, which flourished for more than 4,000 years. Because it flooded annually, the River Nile made the land surrounding it extremely fertile, which enabled the ancient Egyptians to cultivate wheat and other crops. Many Egyptian symbols are rooted in the extremes of the natural environment and in the gods and goddesses thought to influence the natural world and the afterlife. The individual glyphs of the ancient Egyptian pictographic writing system often became symbols that functioned as powerful talismans and amulets.

HEART

Egyptians believed the heart to be the centre of the human being and the seat of wisdom and intelligence. Considered essential for life in eternity, the heart was the only organ left in the body after mummification. At death it was believed that the gods conducted a sacred ceremony during which the heart was weighed against a feather. Maat, the goddess of truth and justice, held the scales. If the scales balanced, the deceased would be invited to enter the underworld. If the heart weighed more than the feather, a monster would devour it.

EYE OF HORUS

Known as *wadjet*, the Eye of Horus represents the left eye of the Egyptian falcon-headed god Horus. As the story goes, Horus's eye was ripped out when he battled his uncle Set to avenge the murder of his father Osiris. The eye was cast into the sky and became associated with the moon. Thoth, the god of the moon, healed the injured eye. From the dark of the moon the eye took 29 days to heal and at the full moon the eye was whole again. Out of love, Horus offered his healed eye to his dead father Osiris, helping to bring him back to life. Thus the Eye of Horus symbolizes sacrifice, wholeness and restorative power.

In many parts of the world today this symbol of the sound eye, or the 'good eye', is worn as an amulet to bring protection from the 'evil eye' – an intrusive, covetous gaze from another person. The Eye of Horus can still be found painted on the prow of fishing boats in Mediterranean countries.

ANKH

The ankh held numerous meanings for the ancient Egyptians, many focused on the concept of 'life'. The ankh represents the life-sustaining elements of water and air, as well as sexual fecundity and the mysteries of death and the afterlife. In Egyptian paintings, gods hold ankh symbols to the noses of pharaohs or queens, symbolizing air as the breath of eternal life. Streams of ankh signs flow down over the monarchs, representing the flow of life-giving water. As a symbol of fertility, the loop of the ankh represents the vagina, and the line below stands for the penis in union with it.

On a spiritual level, the ankh symbolizes the key to hidden knowledge. The loop of the ankh also stands for the eternal soul that has no beginning or end, and the cross represents the actual state of death. The ankh signifies the spiritual initiation that one must go through in order to open the gates of the Kingdom of the Dead and penetrate the meaning of eternal life. The Christian Coptic cross, which is also known as the Gnostic cross, has its origin in the Egyptian ankh.

FETISH

The Egyptian fetish is a stuffed, headless animal skin (usually a great cat or a bull). It is associated with embalming and with the gods Imiut, Anubis and Osiris. The fetish, sometimes with a papyrus or lotus blossom attached to its tail, was hung on a pole and then planted in a pot. It symbolized magical powers captured from the gods for use during funerary rites. Human-made replicas of the fetish crafted out of precious metals have been found in the tombs of the pharaohs.

PALM BRANCH

The palm branch was a practical time-keeping device and a symbol of astrology. Through close observation of the heavens, the Egyptians developed a sophisticated 365-day calendar. They kept track of the days, months and years by placing notches on palm branches, which were also a symbol of longevity. Seshat, the goddess of writing and measurement, was often portrayed holding a notched palm branch on which she calculated the earthly life of the king.

TYET

The tyet – which is also called the Knot of Isis, the Girdle of Isis and the Blood of Isis – is an ancient Egyptian symbol of the goddess Isis. It is often confused with the ankh , except that its arms curve down to resemble the knot that fastens the garments of gods and goddesses. Like the loop of the ankh, the loop of the tyet refers to eternal life, but more specifically to the inexhaustible life force of the goddess Isis from whom all life flows. When made of a red semi-precious stone or glass, the tyet was known as the Blood of Isis, representing the menstrual blood flowing from Isis's womb, bestowing its magical powers and protection on the one who carries the amulet.

Like the ankh, the Knot of Isis is about immortality, but it is also about the spiritual journey that is necessary to realize this state. It reminds the spiritual seeker that they have to unravel the knots that bind one to ordinary life, in order to be free to experience the joys of eternity.

SCARAB

The ancient Egyptians worshiped the scarab or dung beetle as an embodiment of Khepri, the god who maintained the movement of the sun. Khepri is sometimes depicted as a beetle or as a man with a beetle's head. For the Egyptians, the scarab symbolized resurrection and new life. The scarab's rolling of a round ball of dung across the ground was thought to imitate the journey of the sun through the sky. In Egyptian paintings the scarab beetle may be depicted carrying a huge sun on its back.

Because the scarab beetle often lays its eggs in the bodies of dead animals, the ancient Egyptians believed that it was created from dead matter or from the primordial ooze itself. Thus it symbolized the creation of life. Both the god Khepri and the scarab are associated with rebirth, renewal and resurrection – Khepri's name means 'to come into being'. Scarabs are sometimes painted with outstretched falcon wings, symbolizing their role in protection. The carved-stone scarab figure was a popular protective amulet in Egypt.

PAPYRUS

Throughout ancient Egypt, tall papyrus plants covered the marshes of the Nile Delta. The Egyptians depended on this plant to make everyday objects such as boats, mattresses and paper. Thus the papyrus was both a natural symbol of life itself and of the primeval marsh from which it came.

As a perennial, the papyrus symbolized joy, youth and yearly renewal. Papyrus plants, which could grow to 3 metres (10 feet) high, were thought to hold up the sky and consequently many temples were built with papyrus-shaped columns. During the Old Kingdom, the papyrus served as a symbol of Lower Egypt, while the lotus symbolized Upper Egypt.

In hieroglyphics, the papyrus roll had royal connotations and also signified the book and knowledge. To make papyrus rolls, strips of papyrus pith were laid out at right angles on top of each other and pasted together. The rolling and unrolling of the papyrus symbolized two aspects of knowledge: that which was meant for everyone and that which was meant for an inner circle of spiritual initiates. So important was the papyrus plant to the Egyptians that goddesses were depicted holding a stalk as a magical sceptre

SHEN

This hieroglyphic representation of a doubled rope with its ends tied in a straight line, with no beginning or end, was a symbol of eternity, and it also signified protection. It is frequently associated with representations of Heh, the god of eternity, and often forms the base of the notched palm branches held by gods and goddesses, indicating their connection to eternal life.

Sometimes the Shen is depicted with a sun at its centre, symbolizing its solar aspect. In Egyptian paintings, deities in bird form – such as Horus the falcon and Mut the vulture – are shown holding the Shen in their claws.

The word comes from the Egyptian *shenu*, meaning 'to encircle'. In its elongated form, the Shen became a cartouche indicating that the enclosed hieroglyphics referred to a pharaoh or other important figure who was under divine protection. The cartouche symbolized everything that the sun's rays touched, indicating that the king ruled the entire cosmos. The cartouche hieroglyph also appeared on gold finger rings and decorating cartouche-shaped boxes.

SISTRUM

The sistrum, a sacred musical instrument of ancient Egypt, has a frame with small discs that rattle when the instrument is shaken by hand. The basic outline often resembles the ankh, symbolizing life. The head of the goddess Hathor is often depicted on the handle, although the sistrum is also associated with Bastet, the goddess of dance and joy. The instrument produced a soft, jangling sound resembling a breeze blowing through papyrus reeds, a sound that was said to please and placate the gods and goddesses. It was shaken in short, rhythmic pulses to arouse ecstatic movement for religious processions and ceremonies relating mainly to Hathor.

Many of the sistrums in museum collections are inscribed with the names of royal persons and sistrums are depicted in paintings in the hands of royal family members. In Late Period paintings the sistrum is shown held by priestesses of the Hathor cult as they adore the deity face to face. Such intimacy with a god was a female prerogative and use of the sistrum seems to have carried erotic or fertility connotations allied with the cult of Hathor.

DJEW

The Djew, the hieroglyphic sign for mountain, depicts two peaks with a valley running between them. The Egyptians believed that a cosmic mountain range with two peaks named Manu and Bakhu held up the heavens. The double lion god Aker guarded the peaks and protected the sun as it rose and set. The Djew was also a symbol of the tomb and the afterlife, probably because most Egyptian tombs were located in mountainous areas.

AKHET

The Akhet, the hieroglyphic sign for the horizon, is similar to the two peaks of the Djew, but with a solar disc cradled between them. It symbolized sunrise and sunset. For Egyptians, the day began at sunrise, when the goddess Nut gave birth to the sun in her daily affirmation of the triumph of life over death. The sun was thought to sail across the cosmic sky in a boat during the day. It would sink below the horizon at night, to face the demons of the underworld, only to rise again in the morning. As such, the Akhet symbolizes the daily promise of hope and renewal.

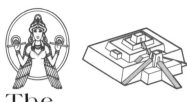

The Mesopotamians

The early Mesopotamian empires of Sumeria, Assyria and Babylon are often referred to as the 'cradle of civilization'. The convergence of the Rivers Tigris and Euphrates, in what is now Iraq, produced rich fertile soil and a supply of water that enabled the growth of agriculture and urban settlements. These settlements started with a collection of houses surrounding a ziggurat, a ceremonial pyramid used for worshipping the divine. In time, these became sophisticated cities that practised agriculture and developed written languages and systems of astronomy and mathematics. Many of the symbols of ancient Assyria and Sumeria revolved around worship of the goddess Ishtar or Inanna, who symbolized the capricious and primal forces of nature that can both create and destroy crops and life.

ISHTAR

The Assyrian moon goddess associated with both fertility and destruction, Ishtar was the most important female deity in Mesopotamia and is associated with many symbols. In her sacred sexual aspect, she is depicted as a nude figure wearing a horned cap with a cone symbolizing the cosmic mountain and an eight-pointed star symbolizing the planet Venus. Her wings designate her status as a stellar goddess.

A crescent worn on her head symbolizes her link to the moon and her seven-coloured necklace represents the seven gates of the underworld. Her girdle depicts the twelve constellations and signs of the zodiac.

Wild and savage, Ishtar was known for her unbridled sexuality and love of war. She is often represented as an armed warrior, sometimes shown riding a lion or standing on a pair of lions.

ZIGGURAT

Common to the Sumerians, Babylonians and Assyrians of ancient Mesopotamia, the temple structures known as ziggurats first appeared in Babylonia around the 3rd millennium BCE. A ziggurat had a square base and was made up of a series of increasingly narrow terraces linked by steep flights of stairs. The ziggurats had up to seven terraces, each painted a different colour, symbolizing the

different planetary heavens. The base represented Saturn and was painted black. The second level was orange, to signify Jupiter. The third was painted red, for Mars. The fourth was golden, for the sun. The fifth was light yellow, for Venus. The sixth was painted blue, to represent Mercury. And the seventh level was silver, signifying the moon. On the top level, priests conducted ceremonies in which sacrifices were made to the gods.

These huge towers were a physical symbol of the enormous need and desire that humans have for connecting with the divine. They were intended to provide a link between heaven and earth and to facilitate the connection between gods and humans. Climbing the ziggurat symbolized the journey from the mundane to the transcendent.

THE TREE OF LIFE

This symbol, which is found in nearly every culture, is a visual representation of the link between the three worlds: heaven, earth and the underworld. The Assyrian Tree of Life, the oldest and most famous of all sacred trees, is associated with worship of the goddess Ishtar . It first appeared on Chaldean cylinders as a pillar crossed by branches and topped by a crescent. The pillar symbolized the human spinal cord or the World Spine. Later, in around the 10th century BCE, the tree became more complex and elegant, with curved branches, scrollwork and beautiful seven-petalled flower forms.

In Babylonia, the Tree of Life was known as a magical tree that grew in the centre of paradise. The Babylonian, Egyptian, Islamic and Kabbalistic Tree of Life , as well as the biblical Tree of Paradise, evolved directly from the ancient Assyrian tree symbol. In all cultures, the Tree of Life is a well-known symbol of fecundity. The serpent and bird, representing the union of matter and spirit, are also associated with the Tree of Life.

NISROCH

The Assyrian god Nisroch was an eagle-headed deity with wings and a body-builder physique. His imposing masculine form represented the absolute power of the king and of the gods. His swift flight and powerful vision symbolized the connection between heaven and earth and between the spiritual and ordinary worlds. In his left hand he holds a water vessel for watering the sacred Tree of Life. This activity symbolized the protection of the land to ensure the royal power of the king and the prosperity of the invincible Assyrian nation.

Nisroch was the beloved god of the Assyrian King Sennacherib who reigned from 704 to 681 BCE and it was in his temple that Sennacherib was murdered by two of his sons. Some scholars have suggested that Nisroch is a representation of Asshur, the patriarch and head of the Assyrian pantheon.

WINGED SPHINX

The Assyrian sphinx, a winged lion with a human head, symbolized royal power. The lion's body represented strength, the wings warned of a swift and ferocious response to attack and the masculine head symbolized royalty. In the form of large stone sculptures, these supernatural beings guarded palace entrances and intimidated invaders as a symbol of overwhelming strength. In addition to warding off potential attackers, sphinxes repelled evil forces and negative energy directed at the king.

MARDUK

The Mesopotamian winged-bull deities symbolized masculine power, protection, authority and the qualities of potency and virility. The deity Marduk appears as a winged bull with a male human face. He gained his patriarchal power by defeating the goddess Tiamat, known as the Dragoness of Chaos and the Primeval Mother of All. Upon his victory he gained 50 names of power. He is known as a Master of Magick, who can banish demons and convey positive energy through the magical use of water. He is a god of healing, regeneration and light, and a firm enforcer of the law.

The Greeks and Romans

Early Greeks and Romans created a civilization that remains the foundation of the Western world today. Their political systems, law, technology, art, literature and language continue to have immense influence on modern Western culture. Greek and Roman religion was polytheistic (worshipping more than one god), and each of the many gods and goddesses expressed archetypal qualities that still find expression today in theatre, literature and film. Other symbols, such as the Roman cornucopia (the horn of plenty), have survived unchanged. The cornucopia has communicated through the ages a complex set of ideas about harvest, plenty, aspirations for wealth and security, thanksgiving for material wealth and the joys of celebration, food and family.

ASCLEPIUS WAND

In ancient Greek mythology, Asclepius, the god of healing, was a practitioner of medicine. The symbol of the wand or rod of Asclepius is associated with astrology and the practice of medicine and consists of a single serpent entwined around a staff. The serpent, which is shedding its skin, is a symbol of rebirth and fertility, while the staff is a symbol of the authority of the god of medicine. Asclepius was so skilled as a healer that he was reputed to have brought patients back from the dead.

CADUCEUS

A winged rod with two snakes wrapped around it, the caduceus is an ancient astrological symbol associated with the Greek god Hermes. It was used by the astrologer-priests in the Eleusinian Mysteries and has since been associated with Gnostic practices and with kundalini yoga. The caduceus is thought to be a symbolic representation of the subtle nerve channels that run up the spine. In the 7th century CE it became associated with astrological medicine and it remains a symbol of medical and pharmaceutical practice today.

OMPHALOS |
LAUREL WREATH |
SCALES OF JUSTICE | PEARL

OMPHALOS

The omphalos, meaning 'navel stone', is a symbol of the centre of the world. According to ancient Greek myth, Zeus sent out two eagles to fly in different directions across the world. Where they met would determine the 'navel' or centre of the world. Omphalos stones used to mark this mythical point were erected in several places around the Mediterranean, the most famous being at Delphi. The omphalos stone may have originated with the 'stone of splendour' associated with the Canaanite god Baal and was said to facilitate communication with the gods.

LAUREL WREATH

A laurel wreath is a circular band made of branches and leaves of the fragrant bay laurel plant. In Greek mythology, laurel symbolizes Apollo, who wears a laurel wreath on his head. The Greeks call laurel *dhafni* because it is also associated with the goddess Daphne. In ancient Greece, wreaths were awarded to victors of the Olympics, poetic contests and military conquests and so the laurel wreath is often seen as a symbol of victory. The term 'poet laureate' has its origin in this ancient Greek practice.

SCALES OF JUSTICE

The scales of justice are associated with Themis, the Greek goddess of divine justice, one of the first oracles at Delphi and an adviser to the god Zeus. She is depicted holding the scales of justice in one hand and a sword in the other, and is sometimes wearing a blindfold. The scales symbolize the weighing of actions and the fair and balanced administration of the law, without prejudice. They also represent the imposing of order and control over the affairs of gods and humans.

PEARL

The pearl – pale, shimmering, lunar, feminine and born in the ocean within the confines of a shell – is associated with hidden knowledge and esoteric wisdom. For the ancient Greeks, pearls were also symbols of love and marriage. The pearl's likeness to a fetus in the womb made it a symbol of the generative powers of the feminine. Also, the pearl symbolized the ideal person of the Greek philosopher Plato (c.428–c. 348 BCE), who required transformation in order to attain perfection.

BEE

In Greek mythology, the bee was a symbol of the soul and was thought to provide a bridge from the natural world to the underworld. The bee was associated with the goddess Demeter and with her daughter Persephone's descent into the underworld. In nature, the bee would seem to disappear in the winter only to return in the spring, and so it became a symbol of resurrection and rebirth. This sacred insect appeared as decoration on tombs as a symbol of the afterlife and some tombs were even made in the shape of beehives.

CERBERUS

Cerberus is the monstrous three-headed dog of Greek mythology. He is said to guard the gates of the underworld (Hades), barring the living from entering and ensuring that the spirits of the dead could enter, but not exit. Hades consisted of several realms, including the Elysian Fields (heaven) and Tartarus (hell). Cerberus, or the Hound of Hades, symbolized a person's fear of the actual hell realms, as well as of the hell realms that exist within one's own psyche. This internal daemon had to be conquered by relying on one's own efforts. The god Herakles tamed Cerberus with the spiritual power of music.

HERCULES' KNOT

The knot of Hercules, created with two intertwined cords, originated as a wedding symbol in ancient Greece. It represented the knotted belt, a symbol of virginity that is worn by the bride and untied by the groom during the ceremony; this custom is the origin of the phrase 'tying the knot'. The knot symbolized the potency of the god Hercules and the legendary 'girdle of Diana' captured from the Amazonian Queen Hippolyta. It was also used as a love amulet.

CUPID

Cupid was the Roman god of love, similar to the Greek god Eros. He is depicted as a winged boy, nude and sometimes wearing a nappy, holding a bow and a quiver of arrows. He symbolizes youth, fickleness and romantic love. He has two sets of arrows: one with gold arrowheads, used to inspire love in the person whose heart he pierces, and the other with lead arrowheads, which provoke hatred. Often he is shown blindfolded, signifying that love is blind.

MEDUSA

According to Greek myth, Athena (also spelled Athene) cursed Medusa because of a sexual transgression, causing anyone who looked upon her to be turned to stone. In reality Medusa was an early serpent goddess, who was worshipped by the women of Lybia and represented female wisdom. She was the destroyer aspect of the Triple Goddess called Neith in Egypt and Athena in North Africa. During the pre-Hellenic period (approximately 2000–1150 BCE) Athena wore the image of Medusa on her breastplate, an indication that she and Medusa were one. However, later classical Greek myth erased the ancient female-wisdom connections of Athena and instead depicted her as an expression of Zeus's wisdom and as having been born out of his head.

CORNUCOPIA

The cornucopia or, horn of plenty, was a symbol of generosity, fruitfulness and happiness in ancient Greek and Roman culture. The cornucopia was associated with many deities, including Copia (goddess of abundance), Bacchus (god of wine), Ceres (goddess of agriculture) and Achelous (the river god), and represented the gifts they bestowed on humans. Later, the cornucopia took on the additional connotations of hard work and foresight resulting in the public good, the bounty of the harvest and the prosperity of all.

TRISKELION

The triskelion, from the Greek word meaning 'three-legged', is one of the oldest symbols known to humankind. The three legs emerging from a central point, representing power, energy and forward motion, can be found on prehistoric rock carvings in northern Italy, on Greek coins and vases from the 6th century BCE and on earlier Mycenean pottery. The version of the triskelion that is a symbol of Sicily has the head of Medusa in the centre. Pliny the Elder said that the triskelion represented the triangular shape of the island and its three bays.

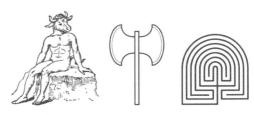

MINOTAUR

This symbol has its origins in the story of Cretan Minos. Wanting to be king, he prayed to Poseidon to send him a snow-white bull as a sign of his approval. A beautiful white bull appeared, but Minos did not sacrifice it as promised. When Poseidon learned about Minos's deception, he made Minos's wife Pasiphae fall madly in love with the bull. Their offspring was a monster called the Minotaur, which had the head and tail of a bull on the body of a man. The Minotaur, who was killed by Theseus, represents the human struggle with one's animal nature.

LABYRS

The labyrs, or 'double axe' symbol, was the emblem of Minoan goddesses, who were depicted holding one in each hand. The labyrs represented a butterfly, as a symbol of transformation and rebirth. The Palace of Knossos was known as the Labyrinth, or the House of the Double Axe, and the labyrs symbol was used extensively as a decorative element in the palace itself. This symbol of the Great Goddess was not intended as a weapon, as it predated the appearance of metal axes by thousands of years.

LABYRINTH

Minos created a labyrinth in which to imprison the Minotaur (see opposite) and every year he locked up seven youths and maidens there for the Minotaur to feast upon. When the hero Theseus learned of these sacrifices, he posed as one of the youths in order to save them. Ariadne, Minos's daughter, fell in love with Theseus and gave him a ball of thread to unravel as he entered the labyrinth. Theseus slayed the sleeping Minotaur at the centre, then led the others to safety by following the thread back to the entrance. The labyrinth symbolizes a journey to the interior of one's soul or psyche.

The Celts

The Celts, an Indo-European people, inhabited large parts of central Europe, Spain, Ireland and Britain between the 5th and 1st centuries BCE. They were animists, believing that everything in the natural world contained spirits, or divine entities, with which humans could establish a relationship. Unlike Greek and Roman culture, Celtic society was predominantly rural and tribal. Power in life came from the otherworld, which was the realm of ancestors and the dead and the dwelling place of the gods and other spirits. Many animals were considered sacred by the Celts and trees were believed to have special powers. Celtic symbols reflect a deep connection to the patterns and energies of the natural world.

LOZENGE

The lozenge is an ancient Celtic female symbol that represents the vulva or womb of the Great Mother. On the feast of St Brighid (1 February), women in parts of Ireland today still make St Brighid's cross, an amulet that consists of a diamond-shaped lozenge of straw woven around a little wooden cross. Every year the crosses are blessed by the priest and hung in houses for protection against fire and lightning. They are also placed in stables for protection of the animals. St Brighid is the direct descendant of the pre-Christian goddess Brighid.

CELTIC CROSS

The Celtic cross – today drawn as a cross superimposed on a circle – has its roots in the pre-Christian, pagan era dating back to 5000 BCE. Although its exact origins are unknown, it may be an early symbol of the Celtic sun god Taranis. In the earliest periods, the cross was drawn entirely within the circle and was without decoration. Later, the cross became larger, the arms were extended and both circle and cross were covered with elaborate decorative elements, including knots, spirals and key patterns.

As a pagan symbol, the Celtic cross combines the female circle and the male cross to form an image of fertility and sexual union. The cross was associated with the four cardinal points of the compass and the flow of time; the circle with the cycles of death and rebirth; and the centre – where time stands still – with the point of entry into the underworld.

The Celtic cross became an emblem of the Church when the Celts converted to Christianity. The cross then symbolized the Crucifixion and the circle stood for Christ's resurrection and eternal life.

CELTIC SPIRALS

Spirals are found in every aspect of nature, from magnetic fields to spiral galaxies and the inner ear. Plants and shells grow in spiral formations and Mother Nature releases her fury in the spiral of the tornado and the hurricane. The Celtic peoples and their ancestors used the spiral to represent the natural world and the spiritual mysteries of life.

The three-pronged Spiral of Life at the entrance to the megalithic passage tomb at Newgrange in Ireland symbolized the sacred cycle of birth, death and rebirth. The initiate would walk round the spiral-marked barrier into the labyrinth sanctuary and then follow the path to its centre; there, heaven and earth were joined.

The Celtic triskelion, a three-pronged spiral within a circle, is also said to represent the Triple Goddess and our triple relationship with the earth, our self and the divine.

CHEVRON

The chevron, a masculine symbol, resembled the arrowheads used by Celtic warriors and represented high rank and military power. It may have represented the shape of a rafter in a building. In ancient Celtic art, the chevron is repeated in bands, forming borders and/or other ornamentation. A simplified form of the chevron, a V shape, is used in modern military insignia to indicate rank or length of service.

KEY PATTERNS

Celtic key patterns are interlocking angular key shapes that are, in effect, straightened spirals. The paths formed by the pattern are constructed on a diagonal grid and turn back on themselves at various angles, symbolizing the winding path of the labyrinth . The key pattern suggests a spiritual journey during which the seeker simultaneously moves toward his or her spiritual centre and that of the universe. At the centre of the labyrinth, called the 'navel' or omphalos, heaven, earth and self are experienced as one.

CELTIC KNOT

A Celtic knot forms a complete loop with no beginning and no end. Celtic knots may be simple or highly complex and are found on crosses, structures, manuscripts and other notable artefacts throughout the Celtic world. Celtic zoomorphic (animal) designs are similar in construction, but the cords terminate in feet, heads or tails. The intricate looping of knot patterns suggests the interconnectedness of all life, eternity and the mysteries of birth, death and reincarnation. The interwoven figures of people and animals signify the intimate connection that the Celts had with the natural world. Some knots were used as magical talismans for protection against earthly threats and evil spirits.

GREEN MAN

The Celtic Green Man, a god of the plant world, is associated with the Celtic belief that gods and spirits lived in trees. His leaf-covered face symbolizes humanity's dependence on the abundance of nature, and the power of the plant world to sustain and renew life. A joyful figure, he was widely celebrated during spring fertility festivals. Carvings of the Green Man were also used for protection from malevolent spirits.

SHEELA-NA-GIG

Often found above church doorways and windows, Sheela-na-Gig is a carved representation of a naked woman with her legs apart, displaying an oversized vulva or yoni. Some believe Sheela-na-Gig represents a pre-Christian pagan goddess, perhaps a fertility figure. Another theory is that she protected against evil. The carvings closely resemble yonic versions of the Hindu goddess Kali, placed above the doors of homes in India for protection. Sheela-na-Gig may depict Kali's Celtic manifestation, Cailleach or Old Woman, a goddess in her crone or destroyer aspect, from whose vulva all life emerges and returns.

The Scandinavians

Gods worshipped by the Norse warriors – the Vikings – included Odin (god of memory and thought), Thor (god of thunder and lightning), Freya (goddess of love and beauty) and Freyr (horned god of fertility). The Vikings also used the longboat as a symbol of speed and supremacy to terrorize their enemies, and in burial rituals as an emblem of the journey to the afterlife. Early Scandinavians also created the runic alphabet, which had both practical and magical uses.

RUNES

'Rune' comes from *runa*, meaning 'secret' or 'hidden'. The runic alphabets (the shortened Scandinavian Fubark is shown here) are both a writing system and a set of magical symbols for divination. Runes were linked to the goddess Idun. Odin received knowledge of the runes by the sacrificial act of hanging himself on the Yggdrasil gallows tree for nine nights.

Examples of runic inscriptions of an everyday nature have been found, ranging from personal and business messages to bawdy and vulgar phrases. However, each letter was also thought to have mystical powers. They symbolized words, ideas and concepts, with specific runes being associated with death, the sun and the moon. Incised on sticks, bones or stones, runes were drawn in groups of three and read for their meaning. They were also used in rituals for writing incantations, and as protective amulets and charms.

F U TH A R K H N I A S T B M L R

Ansuz

Ansuz is the letter A and the fourth letter in the runic alphabet. It represents the mouth, messages and the spoken word. In ancient oral traditions, the spoken word symbolized the vehicle of wisdom and knowledge. Ansuz can refer to advice or instruction received from a doctor, lawyer, teacher or anyone who is more learned than the one questioning the runes. It can indicate an apprenticeship. In its reversed or negative aspect, it can mean receiving bad or biased advice. Combined with other negative runes, Ansuz can indicate the eternal student who never applies knowledge to life.

Sowilo

Sowilo is an S rune, meaning 'sun'. During the 1930s the Nazis adopted the Sowilo rune (which in German is known as the Sigrune or 'victory rune'): two Sowilo runes were crossed to form the Nazi swastika and the SS used a double pair of Sowilo runes as their symbol. In the Norse tradition, the Sowilo rune stands for the sun, represents victory and is associated with Baldr, the god of beauty and light. The Sowilo rune is also believed to bring honour and good luck to those who draw it in a reading.

The Aztecs

The Aztecs achieved political and military dominance during the 14th, 15th and 16th centuries, controlling large parts of Mesoamerica. The Aztec's main city, Tenochtitlan, was founded on the site of present-day Mexico City, where excavations have revealed their remarkable architectural and artistic accomplishments. The Aztecs had a mythological and religious tradition that included the worship of hundreds of deities and the practice of human sacrifice. They met their demise during the 16th century at the hands of the Spanish conquistadors, their population devastated by the diseases brought to the New World. Many contemporary Mexicans are descended from Aztec survivors and today more than one million Mexicans speak Nahuatl, the native Aztec language.

PACHAMAMA

Pachamama is a goddess revered to this day by Mesoamericans. Her name means 'Mother Earth' or 'Mother Universe', and she is a fertility goddess who presides over planting and harvesting. In some regions, people make offerings to her before gatherings by spilling a small amount of *chichi*, or beer, on the floor before drinking the rest. Pachamama's special worship day is called Martes de Challa, when people bury food in the earth and offer her candles and incense; this is celebrated one day before Ash Wednesday in the Christian calendar.

CORN

Maize or corn was a staple food of the ancient Mesoamericans and played a central part in their everyday lives. Flour made from corn provided dough for making flatbreads and the whole corn formed the main ingredient in daily meals. Understandably, corn gods and goddesses formed an important part of the Aztec pantheon. Chicomecoatl, the goddess of nourishment, who is depicted adorned with an elaborate tiered headdress, holds two pairs of ripe, tasselled cobs of corn in her extended hands. Her consort, the god Cinteotl, has yellow skin and maize in his hair. Another deity, the goddess Xilonen, the protector of young maize, is depicted as a virginal girl.

TRIPLE DEATH MASK

The passage of time was one of the main concerns in Aztec society and depictions of it captured their view of life. The Triple Death Mask represented the three phases of the human life cycle: birth and youth, maturity, and old age and death (the end of earthly life). Because these phases of life were believed to repeat, death was followed by lavish ceremonies and preparations for the next life. The Triple Death Mask was worn during religious and divinatory rites and was also used as a grave offering.

AZTEC CALENDAR

The famous Aztec calendar, or Sun Stone, was carved during the 15th century and is today recognized as a symbol of Mexico. The Aztecs dedicated this calendar to their sun god Tonatiuh, whose face appears at its centre. Rings encircled his face, indicating different periods, days and events in the natural and sacred worlds. Both numbers and symbols were used to record time. The Aztecs thought the whole universe was represented in the Sun Stone.

The calendar contained a 365-day civil calendar known as the Xiuhpohualli, which was linked to agriculture and the seasons, as well as a 260-day ritual or sacred calendar, known as the Tonalpohualli. The Xiuhpohualli divided the 365 days into 18 months of 20 days; the five days left over were used for festivities to mark the transition into the new year. The Tonalpohualli was divided into 20 periods of 13 days. Each day had a different symbol dedicated to a specific god. Some gods were considered positive and others negative, and would dictate the energy and mood of the day.

HEART

The Aztecs gave the energy of the heart and blood the name *teyolia*. It was this divine fire that animated humans, giving them their own unique identity. In return, it was thought that teyolia was necessary to strengthen, replenish and sustain the gods. Towards this end, the Aztecs created the ritual of human sacrifice. Every 20 days, in a gruesome procedure, Aztec priests removed the beating hearts of their sacrificial victims, placed them in ritual bowls and offered them to the sun gods.

OLLIN

In the Nahuatl language of the Aztecs, *Ollin* means 'movement'. Four Ollin glyphs frame the centre of the Aztec calendar (Sun Stone) and together they represent the current epoch, which is named Earthquake Sun. The Aztecs believed that the world had been destroyed and recreated four times previously, and that the current epoch will succumb to an earthquake. They attempted to forestall the inevitable by appeasing the gods with rituals and sacrificial ceremonies and with a steady diet of human blood.

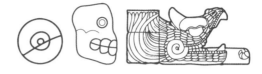

DEATH EYE

In ancient times, life expectancy was short and death was a constant companion. The 'death eye' – which is represented as a straight line cutting through circles – is a common Aztec symbol found on many depictions of the gods. With a strong belief in an afterlife, the Aztecs felt that death was not something to be feared and that to die as a warrior or in a sacrificial rite was honourable. The highest level of paradise was Tonatiuhican, or the House of the Sun, where the souls of warriors and the victims of sacrifice resided.

SKULLS

Skulls are a frequent motif in Aztec art and often represent the skulls of sacrificial victims. Skull racks, or tzompantli, found near temples displayed hundreds of skulls – sometimes real and sometimes carved in stone – to commemorate sacrifices in honour of a god. They were also used as symbols of defeat and humiliation to intimidate subjugated populations. At the Great Temple of the Aztecs, archeologists found a skull rack with at least 240 carved skulls originally painted red.

The Aztec gods of death are often depicted with skull heads. Mictlantechtli has a skull head with large teeth and other deities are shown with skull heads and exposed ribs and bones. Skulls covered in jade were buried along with Aztec nobles, indicating the Aztec belief in an afterlife. The prevalence of skull imagery reflects the Aztec view of death as integral to life; their awareness and acceptance of death was a part of their everyday consciousness.

FEATHERED SERPENT

The cult of the serpent in Mesoamerica is very old. The feathered snake is said to have first appeared in Teotihuacan (not far from present-day Mexico City) in around 150 BCE, as seen in the murals of the ancient city. Quetzalcoatl, the god of sky and earth, is depicted as a serpent covered in the bright-green feathers of the quetzal bird. As an archetype of the divine-human, the feathered serpent symbolizes the union of opposites: heaven and earth, male and female, matter and spirit. It also represents the incarnation of divine light into gross matter/darkness.

CAPTURED CITY

Among rival groups, the Aztecs participated in wars of conquest for the sole purpose of taking captives for human sacrifice to the gods. Captives from neighbouring city-states were sacrificed to their sun god, Huitzilopochtli, whom they believed had chosen the Aztec nation above all others. Aztec warriors were in turn sacrificed to the reigning deity of whatever city captured them. The symbol of the captured city is a person being held by the hair; the name of the captured city is inscribed above the person's head.

The Maya

During their Classic Period from 250 to 900 CE, the Maya produced spectacular art and architecture as well as sophisticated mathematical and astronomical systems. Mayan symbols included many animal forms and a famous calendar. They also produced rich woven textiles decorated with symbols. A common motif was a diamond shape representing the universe and the path of the sun across the sky. Their mathematical system also involved the use of symbols – a dot represented one unit; a straight line, five units; and a shell, zero.

MAYAN CALENDAR

The Mayan calendar is a sophisticated system of 17 different synchronizing calendars. The two most important were the Haab, a 365-day calendar of 18 months made up of 20 days, based on the earth's rotation around the sun; and the Tzolkin, a 260-day calendar tied to the movement of the Pleiades constellation. The Tzolkin, made up of 13 cycles of 20 days, was used to time religious and ceremonial events and for divination. These two calendars were used together to form a 52-Haab cycle called the Calendar Round. The end of the Calendar Round provoked a period of great anxiety and unrest among the Maya, until they were sure the gods were going to grant them another cycle of 52 years.

Longer periods of time were tracked with the Long Count calendar, based on the mythological starting point of 11 August 3114 BCE. Skilled astronomers, the Maya created another calendar for tracking the planet Venus. This cycle was important for choosing auspicious times for coronations and war.

VISION SERPENT

The Vision Serpent is one of the most important of the Mayan serpent gods. During Mayan blood-letting rituals, participants would have a vision of a giant serpent that would permit them entrance to the spirit realm. They would then communicate with whatever the ancestor or god that emerged from the serpent's mouth. Thus, for the Maya, the Vision Serpent was the link between the spirit realm and the ordinary world.

THE SUN

The sun was highly regarded by Mayan civilization because it was thought to bring high crop yields and prosperity to the Mayan people. The sun was the symbol of royal authority and kings were referred to as Kinich Kin, or Sun-Eyed Lord. Kinich Ahau, the sun god, was the patron of the city of Itzamal and was said to visit every day at noon. In Mayan script the Kin glyph means both 'day' and 'sun'. The symbol for Kin, a day-blooming flower, was worn by Kinich Kin.

The Incas

The Incas thrived in South America from 1200 until 1533 CE, when the Spanish conquistador Francisco Pizarro killed the last emperor. The Incas believed they were descended from the sun and worshipped many gods and goddesses, including Pachamama and Pacha Camac – Earth Mother and Earth Father – and the sun god, Inti. For the Incas, the snake represented intellect, the puma courage and the condor balance and life in another dimension. They believed that sacred sites, such as Machu Picchu, were places of power where spiritual energy was amplified.

INCA CALENDAR

Most experts agree that the Inca people developed calendars based on observation of the sun, moon and stars. They used a solar calendar to choose optimal times for planting and harvesting. They also had names for 12 lunar months, although there is no evidence that they had a numerical system for counting time. The emperor god of the Incas, Viracocha, established the 12-month lunar year, with each month beginning with the new moon. His son, Pachacuti, built towers in order to observe the sun, so as to make adjustments to his father's calendar.

One of the primary functions of Machu Picchu, an ancient, secret ceremonial city built high in the Andes, was that of an astronomical observatory. The Inca observed the equinoxes there using shadow clocks such as the Intihuatana Stone, or Hitching Post of the Sun. The Intihuatana 'hitches' the sun when, at midday on 21 March and 21 September, the sun stands directly above the pillar, creating no shadow. Inca legends say that when someone touches his or her forehead to the Intihuatana, it opens that person's vision to the spirit world.

PUMA

The puma is associated with courage and internal strength. It is also connected with the theme of transition and the passage between this world and the underworld (Uku Pacha). The puma is thought to be a child of the earth and thus able to communicate with this realm. At the winter solstice, men dressed in puma skins initiated Inca boys into adult society. Thus the puma was associated with transitions in both the human and natural world. The name of Lake Titicaca means 'meeting place of the pumas'.

CONDOR

The condor, with its 3-metre (10-foot) wingspan, is the world's largest flying bird. The ancient Inca people associated it with Uku Pacha, the underworld, and with the inner worlds of birth, death and fertility. Because it soared high in the sky, it was also identified with mountain peaks and was considered the keeper of lightning. The Inca identified the condor with the solar god Viracocha and worshipped it as a manifestation of the god himself. In Inca lore, the condor symbolizes living on after death in another dimension.

WESTERN AND MIDDLE EASTERN RELIGIONS

Many symbols rooted in Western and Middle Eastern religious traditions are found in contemporary art and culture. They are drawn from Judaism and the mystical Kabbalah, the many forms of Christianity, the esoteric traditions of Freemasonry, Gnosticism and Rosicrucianism, contemporary forms of Wicca and witchcraft, and the ancient culture of Islam. Some symbols are shared, such as the star, which came to represent spiritual illumination and guidance to many traditions. For instance, in Christianity the Star of Bethlehem guided the Magi to Christ's birthplace; in Islam the star is a symbol of ascendancy and of God; and in Freemasonry the blazing star is a symbol of divine providence.

Judaism and the Kabbalah

Judaism has existed for more than 4,000 years. It is a monotheistic religion (worshipping a single God), whose laws and beliefs stem from the covenant that God made with Abraham: that the Jews would be God's chosen people if they followed the laws given to Moses. These laws were recorded in the Torah, the study of which is central to the Jewish faith. The Torah symbolizes the spiritual world and is housed in the Ark of Covenant, an ornate cabinet placed on the wall of the synagogue that faces the holy city of Jerusalem. The Kabbalah, the mystical arm of Judaism, outlines ten spheres, or Sephiroth, through which followers must pass in order to know God. The teachings of the Kabbalah were hidden to the uninitiated through a series of esoteric symbols.

MENORAH

The seven-branched menorah, or candelabrum, is one of the oldest symbols of the Jewish faith, found mostly in temples and synagogues. Ultimately its purpose is not to illuminate the temple, but to act as a physical reminder of Isaiah's commandment to be a light to the world. In the mystical tradition the light of the menorah is said to be drawn from *or ganuz*, the hidden residue of the original light of creation. The roots of the menorah symbol may lie in the ancient Babylonian World Tree or Tree of Life.

STAR OF DAVID

The Star of David is also known as the Magen David, the Shield of David and Solomon's Seal. The six-pointed Jewish star is a universally recognized symbol of Jewish identity and Judaism. Although its origin is unknown, Jewish legend says that the Star of David is modelled on the shield of King David, who unified ancient Israel. To save metal, he went into battle with a round shield made of leather stretched across two interlocking metal triangles. These two triangles symbolize male and female, the union of flesh and spirit, and active and passive principles.

The six points of the Star of David plus the centre give the number seven, which has a particular religious

significance in Judaism, referring to the six days of creation plus the seventh day of rest. The Star of David's structure of 3+3+1 also corresponds to the temple's menorah, which was the more traditional symbol for Judaism in ancient times. In the Kabbalah, the Star of David symbolizes the six directions of space plus the centre.

Mezuzah

A mezuzah is a little scroll containing two short sections from the Torah, placed in a small metal, wooden or ceramic case. It is affixed to the right-hand side of the door frame of Jewish homes to fulfil the biblical commandment to 'inscribe the words of the Shema on the doorposts of your house' – the Shema being an affirmation of Judaism and the declaration of faith in one God. Qualified scribes prepare the parchment with indelible black ink and a special quill pen. As a talisman, the mezuzah symbolizes divine protection and draws God's blessings into the home.

Tallis

In the Torah there is a commandment that Jews should wear tzitzit (strings) on the corners of their garments and so, during prayers, men wear the tallis, a large rectangular shawl fringed with tzitzit. The Talmud states that there are 248 positive and 365 negative commandments that Jews should observe. The sum of the mystical numbers equivalent to the letters that form the word tzitzit is 600; the five knots and eight threads of each fringe make up the other thirteen. By wrapping one's body in a tallis, one dedicates oneself totally to serving God.

Tefillin

Tefillin are leather pouches that are bound to arms and foreheads containing scrolls of Torah passages. At weekday morning services one case is tied to the arm, with the scrolls at the biceps and leather straps extending down the arm to the hand. Another case is tied to the head, with the case positioned on the forehead and the straps hanging down over the shoulders. Appropriate prayers and blessings are recited during this process. The tefillin are removed at the conclusion of the services. As with the mezuzah, the scrolls must be written by hand.

CHAI | TETRAGRAMMATON

CHAI

Chai (pronounced 'hai') is a symbol and word that figures prominently in Jewish culture. It consists of the letters of the Hebrew alphabet Chet and Yud, and means 'living'. According to the system of gematria (the numerology of the Hebrew language), the letters of Chai add up to 18. For this reason 18 is a lucky number in Judaism and many Jews give gifts of money in multiples of 18. For both men and women, the Chai symbol is worn as a medallion around the neck.

TETRAGRAMMATON

YHWH (Yahweh), the sacred name of God in Jewish scriptures, which is also known as the Tetragrammaton. Because Hebrew language was written without vowels in ancient times, God's name was represented by the four consonants Y, H, W, H. The letters may be derived from the Hebrew verb 'to be', and some have understood the original meaning to be 'He-Who-Is', emphasizing God's absolute being, without a beginning or an end. The Tetragrammaton was inscribed on the rod of Aaron and the ring of Solomon. In the Kabbalah, it symbolizes mystical power and the totality of everything.

Universal alphabet

For Kabbalists, the 22 letters of the Hebrew alphabet, the Aleph-Beit, transcend religion, geography and race, and are themselves universal instruments of power. The Hebrew word for 'letter' translates as 'pulse' or 'vibration'. Each letter in the Aleph-Beit is considered a manifestation of the energy of the universe and an ancient key for unlocking the mysteries of the spiritual world.

According to the earliest known book on Jewish mysticism, the Sefer Yetzirah (Book of Creation), God created the universe in the form of Sephiroth, the ten sacred numbers. Then the second set of Sephiroth appeared, the 22 letters of the Hebrew alphabet. Kabbalists believe that these letters, brought together in different combinations, gave rise to both words and matter, creating language and the universe at the same time. Drawing on the divine power residing in the letters, Kabbalists meditate on their forms as portals to sacred truths and to their own souls. Contemplating various combinations of letters releases emotions and brings spiritual realization, positive change and healing into the initiate's life.

ALEPH   BET   GIMMEL

DALED   HAY   VAV

ZAYIN   CHET   YET

YUD   KAF   LAMED

MEM   WUN   SAMECH

AYIN   PAY   TSADEE

KIF   RESH   SHIN

TAF

SEPHIROTHIC TREE

The Sephirothic Tree of Life represents the central system of Jewish Kabbalistic thought. This arrangement of ten interconnected spheres, or Sephiroth, represents the attributes that God created, through which he manifests the physical and mystical universe. Together, the ten Sephiroth provide a step-by-step blueprint of creation and the individual's path to enlightenment. None of the ten Sephiroth are separate from the others; they function in a mystical state of unity within the Tree of Life, forming a more complete view of the perfected whole.

The ten Sephiroth are divided into four realms: Atziluth, the world of the supernatural; Beriah, the creative world of archetypes and ideals; Yetsirah, the world of formation; and finally Assiah, the material world of manifest creation. The Sephiroth are connected by 22 paths or channels, these represent the 22 letters of the Hebrew alphabet. When combined with the 10 Sephiroth, the 22 paths give the number 32, which refers to the 32 Kabbalistic Paths of Wisdom. These 32 paths derive from the first 32 verses of Genesis, in which the Name of God (Elohim) is mentioned 32 times.

Freemasonry

William Schaw, who was made King James VI of Scotland's Master of Works in 1583, was the founder of modern Freemasonry. The Stonemasons who were introduced into the brotherhood were given their mason's mark and were taught the art of building, along with Christian morals and ethics. By the 18th century, Freemasonry included more non-masons than masons and no longer functioned as a true craftsmen's guild, but rather a fraternal organization dedicated to personal and spiritual development.

MASON'S MARK

When stonemasons organized into guilds in the 14th century, they began using unique marks or symbols to identify their work on stone buildings and other public structures. When an apprentice stonemason became a journeyman, he would choose a mark that was his to use for life. The mark was given at a solemn ceremony that was presided over by master stonemasons and concluded with the mark being entered in a record book.

There were two types of marks used by stonemasons: laying-out marks, which were applied at the quarry to expedite construction on site, and signature marks that identified a particular mason. The signature mark is what is generally meant by the term 'mason's mark'. This not only identified the mason in question, but also attested to his character, integrity, reputation and skill. It may have had a practical purpose as a means to claim payment for work completed.

Some special marks may have been used by medieval Freemasons to show that secret principles of geometry were used in the building of a church.

SET SQUARE AND COMPASS

The best-known symbol associated with Freemasonry is the overlapping compass and set square with a letter G in the centre. Since Freemasonry considers itself non-dogmatic, there is no definitive interpretation for the meaning of the set square and compass symbol. However, modern Freemasons suggest that these instruments symbolize a variety of positive virtues, including craft, skill, judgement and discernment. The compass represents the restraint of excess passions and negative emotions, which are circumscribed or controlled by the feminine compass. The right angle of the set square measures the square, a masculine symbol of the earth and the material world. The square also symbolizes fairness, balance and firmness. Something squared is thought to be stable, in alignment with morals and ethics, and suitable as a foundation for building upon. The letter G in the centre is said to refer either to geometry or to God, who is regarded as the Grand Architect of the universe. Some say that the three elements of the Freemasonry symbol refer to the three degrees of Masonry: the Apprentice Degree, Fellow Craft Degree and Master Mason Degree.

BLAZING STAR

The Freemasons' five-pointed star finds its source in the pentagram of Pythagoras. Encoded within the pentagram's structure is the golden ratio, a unique proportion in geometry said to embody divine beauty in form. The Masons used this golden ratio extensively in the design and construction of early cathedrals. For contemporary Freemasons the five-pointed star, or blazing star, is a symbol of light and the mystic centre of the universe. It represents the effort of perfecting the self, with the motivation of illuminating a dark and unconscious world.

EYE IN A TRIANGLE

The eye in a triangle, sometimes referred to as the eye of Providence or the all-seeing eye, is found in Masonic texts and rituals. It symbolizes spiritual knowledge and reminds the lodge member that the Grand Architect of the universe is always judging their words and deeds. The Eye of Providence was a common symbol in the 17th and 18th centuries, when Masonic ritual and symbolism was evolving. It is not surprising that many symbols common to general society made their way into Masonic ceremonies.

BLAZING SUN

Masonic symbols are found as decorative features on many older buildings. The set square and compass are very common, as is the blazing sun – a symbol of the light of God, the universe and eternity. It also represents the journey of the initiate through each of the three principal stations of the Masonic lodge. The face in the blazing sun represents the face of God, as well as the face of the Masonic master.

OUROBOROS

The ouroboros, meaning 'tail devourer', is an ancient symbol depicting a serpent swallowing its own tail and forming a circle. It may have been inspired by the night sky, as some ancient texts refer to a serpent of light residing in the heavens. It is a symbol found in many cultures and generally represents concepts of circularity, unity or infinity. As a Masonic symbol, the ouroboros represents eternity, renewal, love and wisdom. Like the set square and compass, it is used as an architectural decoration on building facades and is incorporated into floors and ceilings.

IMMOVABLE JEWELS

In the American system of Freemasonry, the Immovable Jewels are the square, level and plumb. They are named 'immovable' because they are placed in fixed positions in the lodge – the square to the east, the level to the west and the plumb to the south. The three principal officers of the lodge who sit in these positions wear replicas of the tools.

The square, level and plumb are important and valuable tools for the builder, for without them they cannot work. For the Freemason, these tools symbolize the building of the moral self. The plumb line is a symbol of right, uprightness and proper social and moral behaviour; a Mason is expected to lead an upright life and be of value to his fellow human. The square represents virtue, telling the truth and dealing honestly with others. The level is a symbol of equality and of the need to treat all humans with respect, dignity and understanding.

In the British system the Immovable Jewels are the rough ashlar, the perfect ashlar and the tracing board. The rough ashlar is an unhewn block of stone symbolizing humans in their natural, untutored state, with all their faults and potential for improvement. The perfect ashlar is the educated person, refined and with their mind illuminated or filled with light. The tracing board is a chart of emblems used for illustrating the lectures.

WINDING STAIRS

The image of winding stairs represents the winding stairs of life that a Mason climbs steadily, from birth to their final resting place. It is a symbol of the Masonic process of inner growth and the building of character. The stairs wind to represent the mystery or secret aspects of life's journey. A winding staircase is unpredictable and hides from view that which is around the corner, so it takes courage, faith and determination to continue the climb.

According to Masons, the steps of the winding staircase began at the entrance porch of the Temple. The world of the profane was outside the Temple; the world of the initiated was within its sacred walls. Symbolically, during the Fellow Craft Degree, the initiate advances into the sanctuary, where he finds the winding stair that invites him to ascend. This is the symbol of the Masonic labour of personal self-improvement and character development, and of discipline, research and instruction – the end of which is to be the possession of divine truth.

Wicca and witchcraft

Witchcraft is the practice of using magical powers and supernatural forces for sorcery and divination. Witches are said to have the power to fly, to change shape and to cast spells for good or harm. Wiccans are neo-pagans who are involved in the positive exploration of Wicca (a nature-based religion) or witchcraft in modern times. Modern Wicca precludes the hurting of others and derives power from psychological and psychosomatic effects, rather than from attempts at paranormal or supernatural interventions. Wiccans use personal spells or those handed down from other practitioners.

WITCHES' PENTANGLE

A symbol of witchcraft, the pentangle is a pentagram (or five-pointed star) within a circle. The five points of the pentagram represent the four elements or four directions, with the uppermost point representing the sanctity of Spirit. The pentangle is used in the Wiccan practice of summoning the elemental spirits of the four directions at the beginning of a ritual. Pentangles are also the suit of earth in the Tarot deck.

The outer circle of the circumscribed pentagram is sometimes interpreted as binding the elements together or bringing them into harmony with each other. The pentangle is also associated with the quest for divine knowledge.

WAND

Wiccan practitioners use wands for channelling energy, healing and the casting of spells. Though traditionally made of wood, wands can also be made of metal or crystal. Most practitioners cut a branch from a tree and use it in its natural form, or they may carve and decorate it in order to personalize it. In Wicca, the wand usually represents the element of fire. The wand may have its roots in the drumstick used in ceremonies by tribal shamans or medicine-priests.

ATHAME

The athame is a ritual knife used in witchcraft ceremonies, representing the fire element and the masculine qualities of consciousness, force and action. It often has a double-edged blade, with a black handle that may be inscribed with Wiccan symbols. The athame is used to direct energy and may be employed to cast the magical circle – a circle or sphere marked out during rituals to contain energy, create sacred space or provide protection. When the ritual or ceremony has ended, the practitioner closes the circle by drawing it anticlockwise with the athame.

CHALICE

The chalice is a symbol of the element of water and of the feminine. A chalice represents intuition, psychic ability and the subconscious. It also symbolizes the Goddess, the womb and the female generative organs. It is often used in rituals along with the athame, the symbol of the male principle. The chalice and the blade together symbolize sexual union. The ceremonial use of the chalice is as the holder of ritual liquid, whether this is water to purify the circle or wine for a feast or ritual libation.

HIDDEN PENTANGLE

Hidden pentangles – pentangles that are disguised in intricate designs – can be worn when it is not safe or appropriate to wear a standard witchcraft pentangle. They are sometimes called flower pentangles. These stylized designs can be recognized by other practitioners of the Craft, but are less apparent to others and so less likely to cause problems with a non-pagan family or in the workplace. Wearing a pentangle in any form acts as a protective amulet.

ELEVEN STAR

The eleven star (also called the faery star) is a seven-pointed star associated with practitioners of the Celtic Faery traditions of Wicca. Faery Wiccans focus on gnomes, faeries and sprites and their relation to the natural world. The eleven star is used interchangeably with the pentagram. The seven points represent the seven directions: the four cardinal directions (north, south, east and west) plus above, below and within. They can also represent the seven magical elements: the four alchemical elements (fire, earth, air and water) plus magic, light and life; or seven magical places: the sun, moon, sea, sky, wood, wind and spirit.

DEGREES OF INITIATION

In Wicca, a degree system of initiation marks each individual candidate's level of understanding and proficiency in the Craft. The symbols that accompany each degree represent a special salute in which the hand touches parts of the body in an uninterrupted motion.

FIRST DEGREE

The first degree inducts the witch into the coven and introduces the basic teachings and traditions. The inverted triangle symbolizes the salute: breast, genitals and return to the breast.

SECOND DEGREE (I)

The second degree has two levels. The first part acknowledges progress made following induction and its symbol is an upward-pointing triangle to match the salute: mouth, breast, breast, mouth.

SECOND DEGREE (II)

A down-pointing pentagram represents the second level of the second degree for candidates who have further deepened their knowledge of the rituals and skills. The order of the salute follows the pentagram: genitals, right breast, left hip, right hip, left breast, genitals.

THIRD DEGREE

The third degree is granted to witches who have shown the highest proficiency. The symbol is an upright triangle atop an upright pentangle. The salute is mouth, breast, breast, mouth, genitals, right foot, left knee, right knee, left foot, genitals.

HORNED GOD

The Horned God is the main god that is worshipped in Wicca. He is a composite of horned male nature gods from various traditions, such as the Celtic Cernunnos, the English Herne the Hunter, the Egyptian Osiris, the Greek Pan and the Roman Faunus. As such, the Horned God functions as a universal masculine archetype. He is sometimes referred to as the Great God, who impregnates the Goddess in the autumn and then dies, only to be reborn in spring.

TRIPLE GODDESS

The Triple Goddess, the Horned God's female counterpart, is depicted in several ways. In one of the best-known Wiccan symbols she is represented as the three phases of the moon – a circle or full moon with a crescent moon on each side – but sometimes she is shown as three crescent moons intertwined with each other. The three phases of the moon represent the three stages of a woman's life: maiden, mother and crone. As a goddess, the Triple Goddess is the Wiccan archetype for the feminine aspect of the universe.

EARTH   AIR   FIRE   WATER

ELEMENTAL MARKINGS

55

ESOTERIC AND MAGICAL TRADITIONS

The word 'magic' comes from the Greek *magikos*, referring to the Magians, the Zoroastrian astrologer-priests of ancient Mesopotamia. The practice of magic existed in ancient Egypt, Mesopotamia and Persia, but was restricted to those who were initiated into its mysteries. Because magic was a form of power, over the centuries it remained a hidden practice whose secrets were guarded by various esoteric groups. If an initiate went through a demanding rite of passage, only then would they be introduced to magical symbols and practices that were unknown to outsiders. Alchemy, astrology and ceremonial magic all have their own esoteric symbols.

Alchemy

A precursor to modern-day chemistry, alchemy dates back at least 2,500 years. Its origins can be found in the esoteric practices of Greece and Rome, Persia, India, Mesopotamia, Egypt, China, Japan and Islamic civilizations. This early multi-disciplinary practice combined art, chemistry, metallurgy, medicine, astrology, and mysticism. Viewed by outsiders as the practice of creating gold, alchemy was in reality focused on spiritual enlightenment. Carl Jung compared it to the process of individuation, in which a person explores the dark material of the unconscious mind, integrates it on a conscious level and achieves psychological maturity and spiritual insight. Because the Church deemed alchemy heretical, alchemists used symbols to disguise their work.

PHILOSOPHER'S STONE

This representation of humankind's wholeness symbolizes the fierce desire to be one mystical union with God, within one's own soul. In alchemy, the Philosopher's Stone is not a physical stone, but a legendary substance capable of turning base metal into gold. Ultimately, this was the most sought-after goal in alchemy. It was also believed to be an elixir of immortality and, once made or achieved, could never be lost. The Philosopher's Stone thus became a metaphor for the inner potential of a human being to evolve from a lower state of imperfection (symbolized by base metals) to a higher state of enlightenment and perfection (symbolized by gold). In this view, the transmutation of metals and the spiritual transmutation, purification and rejuvenation of the body were one and the same. The Philosopher's Stone may be represented abstractly or by a pair of lions or a man and woman riding on lions.

HERMES TRISMEGISTUS

Hermes Trismegistus is the combined form of the Egyptian god Thoth and the Greek god Hermes, both gods of writing and magic in their respective cultures. During the Renaissance, the Greek writings attributed to Hermes Trismegistus from the 2nd and 3rd centuries CE were compiled into the *Corpus Hermeticum* and became known as *Hermetica*. The original source of these writings, said to contain secret wisdom, may have been an Egyptian movement that represented a marginal sect within the Greco-Roman cultures. Most of the texts are presented as a dialogue (a popular teaching form in ancient times), in which Hermes-Thoth enlightens a confused disciple. The subject matter deals with alchemy, magic and concepts reminiscent of Gnosticism and Neoplatonism.

The recovered Hermetic writings gave rise to mystical practices all over the world. Hermetic philosophy provided the individual with a way to transform one's base physical nature into higher realms. Today, the 'Hermetic tradition' refers to alchemy, magic, astrology and other occult subjects and practices.

MATERIALS USED IN THE ALCHEMICAL PROCESS

Alchemists make use of the innate qualities of the huge range of materials they employed in their experiments. Each substance is represented by an alchemical symbol. The following pages provide examples of some of these substances and symbols.

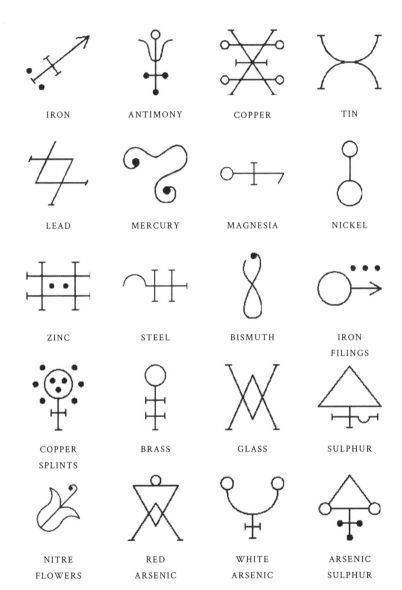

IRON	ANTIMONY	COPPER	TIN
LEAD	MERCURY	MAGNESIA	NICKEL
ZINC	STEEL	BISMUTH	IRON FILINGS
COPPER SPLINTS	BRASS	GLASS	SULPHUR
NITRE FLOWERS	RED ARSENIC	WHITE ARSENIC	ARSENIC SULPHUR

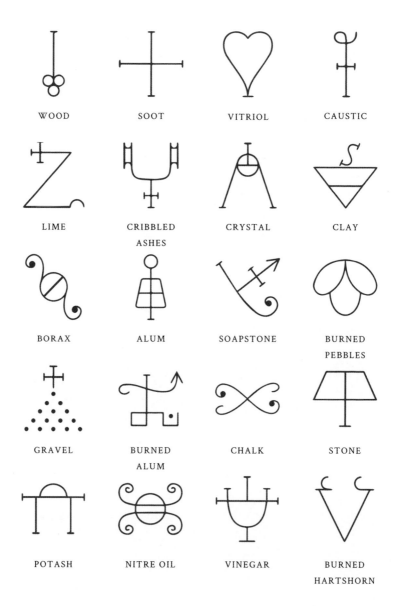

WOOD

SOOT

VITRIOL

CAUSTIC

LIME

CRIBBLED
ASHES

CRYSTAL

CLAY

BORAX

ALUM

SOAPSTONE

BURNED
PEBBLES

GRAVEL

BURNED
ALUM

CHALK

STONE

POTASH

NITRE OIL

VINEGAR

BURNED
HARTSHORN

URINE

VERDIGRIS

GINGER

MANURE

EGGSHELLS

SUGAR

WINE SPIRIT

YELLOW
WAX

HONEY

ROCK SALT

SEA SALT

CINNABAR

Astrology

Since ancient times, humans have watched the skies and observed the movement of the sun, moon and stars. Knowledge of the skies combined with mythology created the complex system known as astrology. Early astrologers developed intricate systems of glyphs, or symbols, to explain the movement of the sun, moon and planets through the zodiac. The glyphs shown on these pages come from medieval manuscripts.

ARIES

Aries (21 March–19 April), the first sign of the zodiac, is a masculine, extroverted sign. A fire sign, it is one of the four cardinal signs representing action (Aries, Cancer, Libra and Capricorn) and is ruled by the planet Mars. In mythology, Aries is associated with Theseus and the Minotaur. Those born under Aries take the initiative in business and in life and perform courageous acts. The symbol of Aries represents the head and horns of a ram and originates from the cluster of stars in the northern sky that make up the 'head' of the Aries constellation.

TAURUS

Taurus (20 April–20 May), the second sign of the zodiac, is considered a feminine, introverted sign. An earth sign, it is one of four signs related to stability (Taurus, Leo, Scorpio and Aquarius) and is ruled by the planet Venus. In mythology, it is associated with Aphrodite. Its symbol, which looks like bull's horns, is also one of the alchemical symbols for rock salt. Taureans are grounded, responsible, affectionate and sensual.

GEMINI

Gemini (21 May–21 June), the third sign of the zodiac, is considered a masculine, extroverted sign. An air sign, it is one of four mutable signs concerned with communication (Gemini, Virgo, Sagittarius and Pisces) and is ruled by the planet Mercury. In mythology, Gemini is associated with the god Hermes/Mercury. Gemini's symbol is the twins and those born under this sign often feel they have a duality of purpose or that they have two separate destinies pulling them in two different directions. Geminis are often known for their open-mindedness and outgoing, inquisitive nature. They are good communicators and multi-taskers.

CANCER

Cancer (22 June–22 July), the fourth sign of the zodiac, is considered a feminine, introverted sign. It is also a water sign, one of four cardinal signs and is ruled by the moon. Cancer's symbol is the crab and it is linked with illumination and insight. In mythology, Cancer is associated with the god Hercules. Cancer individuals are known for their sensitive, emotional natures and need their hard shells to retreat into when they become overwhelmed. They are renowned for their nurturing and protective qualities.

LEO

Leo (23 July–22 August), the fifth sign of the zodiac, is a masculine, extroverted sign. A fire sign, it is one of the four fixed signs and is ruled by the sun. Its symbol is the lion. Leo individuals are said to have the greatest intensity of the fire signs. In mythology they are associated with the god Apollo and the Nemean lion. They are less impulsive than Aries individuals and not as prone to wanderlust as those born under a Sagittarius sun. They make excellent leaders, exuding regal authority and a controlled but powerful presence.

VIRGO

Virgo (23 August–22 September), the sixth sign of the zodiac, is a feminine, introverted sign. It is an earth sign, one of the four mutable signs and is ruled by the planet Mercury. Its symbol is the virgin. In mythology, Virgo is identified with Persephone, daughter of Demeter, the goddess of agriculture. Persephone was the goddess of innocence and purity, but later on became the queen of the underworld, when she was abducted by Hades. Virgo is associated with precision, detail and transitions.

LIBRA | SCORPIO |
SAGITTARIUS | CAPRICORN

LIBRA

Libra (23 September–23 October), the seventh sign of the zodiac, is a masculine, extroverted sign. It is an air sign, one of the four cardinal signs and is ruled by the planet Venus. Its symbol represented by the scales. Libra is often associated with Themis, the Greek goddess of justice. Librans love harmony, justice and equality and they weigh up their choices before taking action. They are diplomatic, fair, idealistic, cooperative and peace-loving.

SCORPIO

Scorpio (24 October–22 November), the eighth sign of the zodiac, is a feminine, introverted sign. It is a water sign, one of the four fixed signs and is ruled by the (now ex-) planet Pluto. Its symbol is the scorpion. It is associated with birth, death, transformation, sexual relationships and the occult and psychic matters. In mythology, Scorpio is linked to Hades, ruler of the underworld. Those born under the sign of Scorpio are intense, loving, powerful, secretive, passionate and loyal.

SAGITTARIUS

Sagittarius (23 November–21 December), the ninth sign of the zodiac, a masculine, extroverted sign. It is a fire sign, one of the four fixed signs and is ruled by the planet Jupiter. Its symbol is the archer. In mythology, Sagittarius is associated with the centaur Chiron and the Greek god Zeus. Sagittarians are linked with foreign travel, religion, higher education and whatever expands the mind or experience. They are freedom-loving, adventurous, honest, idealistic and concerned with morality.

CAPRICORN

Capricorn (22 December–19 January), the tenth sign of the zodiac, is a feminine, introverted sign. It is an earth sign, one of the four cardinal signs and that is ruled by the planet Saturn. Its symbol is the goat. In mythology, Capricorn is associated with the gods Saturn and Zeus. Capricorns are known to be practical, disciplined, very methodical and organized. They can also choose to follow a path to higher spiritual awareness, leaving the material world behind.

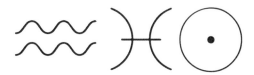

AQUARIUS

Aquarius (20 January–18 February), the eleventh sign of the zodiac, is a masculine extroverted sign. It is an air sign, one of the four fixed signs and is ruled by the planet Uranus. Its symbol is the water carrier. In mythology, Aquarius is associated with Odysseus and the Trojan War. Aquarians are known to be strong-willed, magnetic, free-spirited, intelligent, intuitive, idealistic and somewhat detached emotionally. They can be spontaneous and even erratic, but also inflexible due to their fixed nature.

PISCES

Pisces (19 February–20 March), the twelfth sign of the zodiac, is a feminine, introverted sign. It is a water sign, one of the four mutable signs and is ruled by the planet Neptune. Its symbol is a pair of fish swimming in opposite directions, held together by a cord. In mythology, Pisces is associated with the story of Aphrodite and Eros. Pisceans are gentle, good-natured, compassionate, spiritual, impractical and sometimes naive. They can be dreamy and escapist, but are very likeable.

SUN

In astrology, the sun is considered one of the planets. It is the star at the centre of our solar system, around which the earth and the other planets revolve. Every day, the sun appears in a slightly different place in the sky, reflecting the earth's changing orbit around it. The sun's arc across the sky is larger at latitudes further north or south from the equator, causing differences in the lengths of days, nights and seasons. The sun travels through the 12 signs of the zodiac each year and its position on a person's birthday determines their sun sign. In Western mythology, the deity of the sun is Apollo.

Astrologically, the sun symbolizes the conscious ego, the self and its expression. It is yang, masculine, paternal and represents life force. Qualities such as personal power, assertiveness, pride, authority, leadership, spontaneity, health and vitality are attributed to the sun. Most importantly, the quality of a person's creative expression, from parenting to work, has its origin in their sun sign.

MOON

The sun sign in which your moon is present when you are born is known as your moon sign and the characteristics of that sun sign affect your moon's expression. Astrologically, the moon is often associated with the emotions, the unconscious, memories, changing moods and the ability to react and adapt to other people and a range of different surroundings and environments.

While the sun rules your individuality, the moon rules the deeper aspects of your personality, including its hidden aspects. The moon is yin, feminine, maternal, receptive and represents the need for security. It is associated with the breasts and the ovaries in women and with their monthly menstruation.

The moon's gravity has a powerful effect on the earth, stabilizing its orbit and causing the ebb and flow of the tides. The moon is known for its different phases, waxing and waning as it orbits the earth in about 28 days.

In mythology, Artemis, the twin sister of Apollo, represents the moon. Artemis is the goddess of the hunt and also the defender of wild animals and children. The goddess is often depicted with a crescent moon on her forehead and carrying her bow and arrows.

MERCURY

Mercury is the ruling planet of Gemini and Virgo. In mythology, Mercury was the speedy messenger of the gods and the planet Mercury – equally speedy – takes only 88 days to orbit the sun. In astrology, Mercury represents communication, rationality, reasoning and adaptability. It is the planet of education, neighbours, siblings, cousins and messages of all kinds. Mercury is also linked to newspapers, journalism, writing, the Internet and information-gathering in general.

VENUS

Venus is the ruling planet of Taurus and Libra and the second-brightest object in the night sky after the moon. In Roman mythology, Venus was the goddess of love and beauty. The planet Venus orbits the sun in 225 days. Astrologically, Venus represents harmony, beauty, feeling, affections and the desire to merge with others. It symbolizes pleasure, sensuality, romance, sex, marriage and partnerships of all kinds. When Venus is in Taurus it is expressed through the physical senses, while in Libra it is expressed as an intellectual sense of harmony and balance.

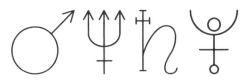

MARS

Mars is the ruling planet of Aries. Before the discovery of Pluto, Mars was also considered the ruler of Scorpio. Mars was the violent Roman god of war. The planet Mars orbits the sun in 687 days. Astrologically, it is associated with masculinity, confidence, ego, energy, passion, drive, aggression, sexuality, strength, ambition and competition. The energy of Mars can be constructive or destructive, so it is important to harness its forces for good. Stamina, ambition and achievement can be its positive expressions.

NEPTUNE

Neptune is the ruling planet of Pisces. In Roman mythology, Neptune was the god of the sea. Discovered in 1846, the planet Neptune takes 165 years to orbit the sun. In astrology, Neptune is associated with idealism, compassion, spirituality, mysticism, imagination, psychic phenomena and altered states of consciousness; and, in its negative aspect, with confusion, deception and drugs and alcohol. Neptune rules the world of illusion – film, TV, theatre and fashion. It invites individuals under its influence to deepen their spirituality in a positive way, through trance, music or dance.

SATURN

Saturn is the ruling planet of Capricorn and, before the discovery of Uranus, of Aquarius. Saturn was the Roman god of agriculture and civilization. The planet Saturn takes 29.5 years to orbit the sun. Astrologically, Saturn is associated with limitation, restrictions, boundaries, practicality, reality and long-term planning. Discipline and responsibility are central to Saturn. The return of Saturn, about every 30 years, is said to mark significant changes in each person's life. Saturn reminds us of the limitations of time and the need to manage it well.

PLUTO

Pluto is the ruling planet of Scorpio. In Roman mythology, Pluto was the god of the underworld and of wealth. Pluto takes 248 years to orbit the sun. Astrologically, Pluto is associated with destruction that ushers in renewal and transformation. It is linked with power, personal mastery, the depths of the unconscious, the collective and what is hidden from view. In its negative aspect it governs crime, corruption, obsession, coercion, terrorism and dictatorships. In its positive aspect it supports transcendence, redemption and rebirth.

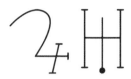

JUPITER

Jupiter is the ruling planet of Sagittarius and, before the discovery of Neptune, also the ruler of Pisces. In Roman mythology, Jupiter was the ruler of the gods and his symbol was the thunderbolt. The giant planet Jupiter takes 11.9 years to orbit the sun. In astrology, Jupiter is linked to growth, expansion, prosperity, good fortune, leisure, wealth, religion, philosophy, long-distance travel and higher goals. Although it can feel judgemental, Jupiter is more often a benevolent planet that wants individuals under its influence to grow and flourish.

URANUS

Uranus is the ruling planet of Aquarius. In Greek mythology, Uranus was depicted as the personification of the sky who made love to Gaia, the earth. As the planet Uranus rotates on its side, it stands for the unconventional. Uranus takes 84 years to orbit around the sun. Having no use for tradition or the status quo, it sides with genius, individuality, unconventional ideas, new discoveries computers, cutting-edge technology, as well inventions and freedom of expression. Uranus supports humanitarian ideals, equality, freedom, creativity, as well as political rebellions and revolutions.

THE MOON'S NODES

The moon's nodes are the two points in its orbit that intercept the earth's path around the sun. Node signs are always opposite one another in the zodiac wheel and always appear in pairs. The north node is known as the Dragon's Head and the south node as the Dragon's Tail. In astrology, nodes are significant because they indicate one's capacity for personal and spiritual growth.

The ascending north node produces positive influences and indicates the path of the moon moving from south to north. It represents the future, the direction in which an individual's life is heading and the lessons that they need to learn. The descending south node marks the intersection of the moon travelling from north to south. It is associated with negative, hindering influences. It represents the past and indicates issues from former lives that need to be addressed.

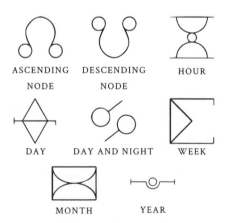

ASCENDING NODE   DESCENDING NODE   HOUR

DAY   DAY AND NIGHT   WEEK

MONTH   YEAR

Aspects

These are key to the interpretation of an astrological chart. Aspects are the angles between two or more planets that may be in the sky at the time of one's birth and considering them helps to determine the meaning of those planetary relationships. The major aspects are conjunctions (0 degrees apart or planets right next to each other), sextiles (60 degrees apart), squares (90 degrees apart), trines (120 degrees apart) and oppositions (180 degrees apart). Squares and oppositions are called hard aspects and represent challenges to be overcome. Sextiles and trines are called soft aspects and are considered to be beneficial. Conjunctions can be either positive or negative, depending on the planets involved.

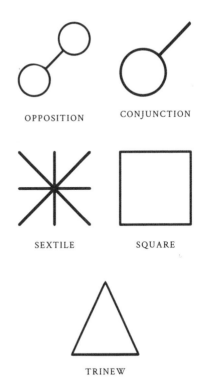

OPPOSITION

CONJUNCTION

SEXTILE

SQUARE

TRINEW

Ceremonial magic

Ceremonial magic enjoyed a renewed popularity after the practitioner Aleister Crowley (1875–1947) created his own system of occult magic. He emphasized the development of personal power and will, and the practice of conjuring up spirits or entities to assist the magician. He devised complex rituals for focusing the mind to allow the magic to take place and to protect the magician from the conjured entity and spirits. Purification practices and the donning of ceremonial robes preceded the ritual. Numerous symbolic and magical objects are used in the production of ceremonial magic.

THE MAGICAL SEALS OF THE SEVEN ANGELS OF THE SEVEN DAYS OF THE WEEK

During the Middle Ages magicians would conjure up spirits, who would then do whatever the magician wanted them to do. The magician would perform the summoning ritual within a magic circle to protect himself from the malevolence of the spirit. Clothing and tools were inscribed with Words of Power, or seals, which contained the names of angels and archangels that were known only to the magician. The day the ritual was performed determined which seal was used.

Raphael. ♈   ♊ ♍
   ⌁⊙┼⊕⊞══✴ **Raquie.**

RAPHAEL (WEDNESDAY)

Michael.   ☉   ♌
♈┼⊕ ⚌Ⅹ∨ **Machen.**

MICHAEL (SUNDAY)

Sachiel. ♃   ⇸ ♓
⌁⊡ ♈ ♈ **Zebul.**

SACHIEL (THURSDAY)

Gabriel.   ☽   ♋
⌐♭♭⊞♫♏ **Shamain.**

GABRIEL (MONDAY)

Anael.   ♀   ♎ ♉
♉   ∿ **Sagun.**

ANAEL (FRIDAY)

Samael.   ♂ ♈. ♏.
⊞ ♐⊕ **Machon.**

SAMAEL (TUESDAY)

Caßiel   ♄   ♑
⊳ ♈♪ ♉ ≈

CASSIEL (SATURDAY)

71

Ceremonial markings

During ceremonies, magicians would mark their clothing and tools, such as wands and knives, with protective signs and symbols. Each item of clothing or tool had its own seal.

SYMBOLS FOR MARKING THE ASSISTANTS' CROWNS

SYMBOLS FOR MARKING THE SWORD

SYMBOLS FOR MARKING THE SHOES

SYMBOLS FOR MARKING THE KNIFE WITH A WHITE HILT

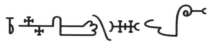

SYMBOLS FOR MARKING THE MAGICIAN'S ROBES

SYMBOLS FOR MARKING THE KNIFE WITH A BLACK HILT

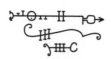

SYMBOLS FOR MARKING THE ASSISTANTS' GARMENTS

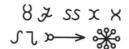

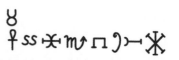

SYMBOLS FOR MARKING THE SCIMITAR

72

SYMBOLS FOR MARKING THE SHORT LANCE

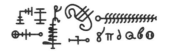

SYMBOLS FOR MARKING THE SILKEN CLOTH

SYMBOLS FOR MARKING THE DAGGER
AND PONIARD

SYMBOLS FOR MARKING THE VIRGIN
PARCHMENT

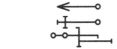

SYMBOLS FOR MARKING THE BURIN

✠ TETRAGRAMMATON ✠ JEHOVA ✠

SYMBOLS FOR MARKING THE NECRO-
MANTIC TRIDENT

SYMBOLS FOR MARKING THE BELL
ASSISTANTS' GARMENTS

SYMBOLS FOR MARKING THE BATON

SYMBOLS FOR MARKING THE WAND AND
STAFF ASSISTANTS' CROWNS

SYMBOLS FOR MARKING THE BAGUETTE

SYMBOLS FOR MARKING THE TRUMPET

SYMBOLS FOR MARKING A MAGIC CANDLE

POINT

ROUND

Characters of good spirits

Good spirits bring benevolent energies to the ceremonies and rituals of magicians and witches. Invoked to bring positive forces to assist in the creation of magic, these good spirits include nature and guardian spirits.

STARRY

PERPENDICULAR

HORIZONTAL

OBLIQUE

BOWED LINE

WAVING LINE

TOOTHED

INTERSECTION RIGHT

INHERENT

ADHERENT SEPARATE

OBLIQUE INTER-SECTION SIMPLE

MIXED

MANIFOLD

PERPENDICULAR RIGHT DEXTER

74

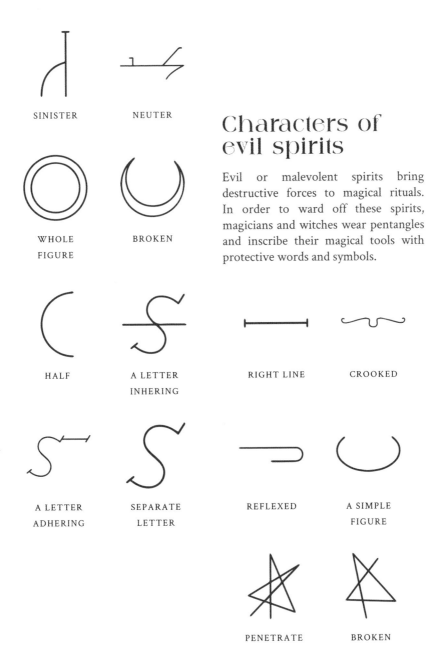

SINISTER

NEUTER

WHOLE
FIGURE

BROKEN

HALF

A LETTER
INHERING

RIGHT LINE

CROOKED

A LETTER
ADHERING

SEPARATE
LETTER

REFLEXED

A SIMPLE
FIGURE

PENETRATE

BROKEN

Characters of evil spirits

Evil or malevolent spirits bring destructive forces to magical rituals. In order to ward off these spirits, magicians and witches wear pentangles and inscribe their magical tools with protective words and symbols.

INVERSED

FLAME

WIND

WATER

FLYING
THING

CREEPING
THING

SERPENT

EYE

HAND

FOOT

CROWN

CREST

HORNS

SCEPTRE

SWORD

SCOURGE

A RIGHT
LETTER

RETROGRADE

4	9	2
3	5	7
8	1	6

SQUARE OF
SATURN

Magic squares

Magic squares work by enclosing or trapping an entity or power, by surrounding it with a collection of numbers in a particular relationship. Some magic squares are made up of symbols of planets, metals or magic words. The numerals and letters that make up the name of God are believed to be especially powerful. One magic square is made up of the Latin sentence *Sator arepo* tenet opera rotas, meaning 'The sower at his plough controls the work'. In magical squares where the numbers on vertical and horizontal lines always add up to the same number, the result is called the 'constant'.

4	14	15	1
9	7	6	12
5	11	10	8
16	2	3	13

SQUARE OF
JUPITER

11	24	7	20	3
4	12	25	8	16
17	5	13	21	9
10	18	1	14	22
23	6	19	2	15

SQUARE OF
MARS

6	32	3	34	35	1
7	11	27	28	8	30
19	14	16	15	23	24
18	20	22	21	17	13
25	29	10	9	26	12
36	5	33	4	2	31

SQUARE OF THE
SUN

8	58	59	5	4	62	63	1
49	15	14	52	53	11	10	56
41	23	22	44	48	19	18	45
32	34	38	29	25	35	39	28
40	26	27	37	63	60	31	33
17	47	46	20	21	43	42	24
9	55	54	12	13	51	50	16
64	2	3	61	60	6	7	57

SQUARE OF
MERCURY

22	47	16	41	10	35	4
5	23	48	17	42	11	29
30	6	24	49	18	36	12
13	31	7	25	43	19	37
38	14	32	1	26	44	20
21	39	8	33	2	27	45
46	15	40	9	34	3	28

SQUARE OF VENUS

S	A	T	O	R
A	R	E	P	O
T	E	N	E	T
O	P	E	R	A
R	O	T	A	S

SQUARE OF *SATOR AREPO*
TENET OPERA ROTAS

37	78	29	70	21	62	13	54	5
6	38	79	30	71	22	63	14	46
47	7	39	80	31	72	23	55	15
16	48	8	40	81	32	64	24	56
57	17	49	9	41	73	33	65	25
26	58	18	50	1	42	74	34	66
67	27	59	10	51	2	43	75	35
36	68	19	60	11	52	3	44	76
77	28	69	20	61	12	53	4	45

SQUARE OF THE MOON

ANIMALS

Humanity's fascination and sense of kinship with animals dates from earliest times. Animals were companions as well as sources of food, shelter and clothing. In pre-dynastic Egypt the gods were animals – and the animal figures found on the walls of Egyptian tombs and the pervasive use of animal symbols in Greco-Roman culture attest to the profound nature of this highly interdependent relationship. The Celts and their Druid priests continued to honour the intimate relationship between humans and animals. In the New World, shamanic Native American cultures revere their relationship with animals and esteem their wisdom.

Mammals

Many Native American creation stories credited animals with the origin of the universe, because animals were considered ancient and humans relatively new to the earth. So it was only natural to turn to animals for knowledge and wisdom. On many totem poles the human figure is found at the bottom rather than at the top, reflecting the human responsibility to honour and care for all other species. Totems were animal mentors and protectors, and each clan or tribe had special relationships with particular animals. Elsewhere, later European and Middle Eastern cultures split animals from humans, with the Hebrews and the Roman Catholic Church forbidding the worship of animals.

BULL

In ancient cultures the Palaeolithic goddess, the Venus of Laussel, is shown holding a crescent-shaped bull horn, while the Egyptian god Osiris was often depicted with the head of a bull. The bull is both a solar and a lunar creature. His male fertility and his fiery temperament make him the masculine sun god in many ancient cultures. However, the bull's crescent-shaped horns link him to moon worship. The moon goddess Astarte often rode a bull. The bull represents valour, bravery, generosity, strength and fortitude.

COW

Nut, the Egyptian goddess of the night sky, was often represented as a cow, as was the Egyptian goddess Hathor. In many cultures the cow represents the Great Mother, the earth, love, nurturing, warmth and abundance. Cow deities, such as Nandini, the wish-fulfilling cow, are popular in Vedic literature. In Hinduism, the cow is believed to be a treasure produced from the cosmic ocean by the gods. Because cows are still considered sacred in India today, they are given the freedom to wander wherever they choose. Their horns are often decorated with flowers and coloured ornaments, as a sign of respect and affection. The East African Maasai people also consider their cows as gifts from God. According to Norse creation myths, the cow Adumla was the first creature to emerge, and created the first man by licking him out of a salt block.

BUFFALO

At 900kg (2,000lb) and 1.8 metres (6 feet) tall at its humped shoulders, the American buffalo or bison is an impressive animal. Before every hunt, Native Americans praised the buffalo with a tribal ritual dance. This animal supplied virtually everything that the Plains people needed: food, clothing, tools and housing materials. The animals were called 'buffalo people' by some tribes and revered for their power and the good fortune they brought. The hide of the rare white buffalo became a sacred talisman and a priceless possession.

DOG

The dog, the emblem of faithfulness and guardianship, has been one of the most widely kept working and companion animals in human history. Dogs embody courage, playfulness, sociability and intelligence, and possess excellent hunting skills. The Talbot, an English hunting dog, was found on the coats of arms of famous hunting families. In 13th-century France a greyhound was revered as St Guinefort. The Greco-Romans, who described those from elsewhere as 'dog-headed' peoples, depicted St Christopher, who was an outsider from the tribe of the Marmaritae, with the head of a dog.

CAT

Cats are inscrutable, nocturnal creatures. The ancient Egyptians and the early Christians revered the cat, but they were persecuted as the familiars of so-called witches during the Middle Ages and became anathema to the Church. They symbolize independence, and the merging of the spiritual with the physical and of the psychic with the sensual. Cats represent wisdom and manifest confidence and self-assurance when confronted. They reach the height of their powers at night and are associated with the moon.

RABBIT

In fairy tales the rabbit appears as the trickster archetype, using its cunning to outwit enemies. The rabbit can also symbolize fertility, innocence and youthfulness. In China and Japan it is associated with the moon, because the dark areas towards the top of the full moon suggest the form of a rabbit. In China, figures of white rabbits are made for the Moon Festival. In North American folklore, a rabbit's foot is carried as a charm on key chains for good luck.

PIG

In many cultures the pig is a fertility symbol, but also represents negative qualities such as gluttony, greed, lust, anger and the unclean. In some traditions, the sow is associated with the Great Mother. Swine were sacrificed at harvest time to Ceres and Demeter in ancient Greece, in their form as fertility goddesses. In Buddhism, the Diamond or Adamantine Sow is Vajravarahi, Queen of Heaven. In Catholicism, St Anthony is the patron saint of swineherds.

GOAT/RAM

In Egypt, the goat was a symbol of nobility. The horned goat god Pan was one of the oldest Greek deities, associated with nature and sexual energy. Christianity has depicted Satan as having the body parts and horns of a goat, possibly because in the Middle Ages the symbol of lust was a buck in rut. In Chinese astrology, the goat is associated with shyness, introversion, creativity and perfectionism. In fairy tales and folklore, fauns and satyrs are mythological creatures that are part ram or goat and part human.

SHEEP

The female sheep was associated with the Celtic goddess Brigit or Brighid and her spring festival Imbolc, meaning 'ewe's milk'. Christ carrying a lamb or a sheep on his shoulders symbolizes the soul of the deceased being borne by him into heaven. Sheep represent the flock or congregation of Christ, who is known as the Good Shepherd. Christ is also portrayed as the Sacrificial Lamb of God or Agnus Dei. In the Abrahamic faiths, Abraham, Isaac, Jacob, Moses and King David were all shepherds. In Chinese folklore, because of the way a lamb dances around its mother, it is a symbol of respect and love for parents. Sheep are key symbols in fables and nursery rhymes such as 'The Wolf in Sheep's Clothing' and 'Baa Baa Black Sheep'. In Europe, a black sheep is considered a sign of good luck. In the English language, calling someone a sheep suggests that they are timid and easily led.

ASS/DONKEY

Asses and donkeys have accompanied humans as pack animals and companions since around 6000 BCE. The ass was a symbol of the Greek wine god Dionysus, the Egyptian god Ra and Jesus Christ. Asses and donkeys have a reputation for stubbornness, but this is a result of their sense of self-preservation and their own best interests. They are highly intelligent, cautious, friendly, playful and eager to learn. Folk tales tell of the donkey hiding in various disguises, but giving itself away with its loud braying.

HORSE

Horses personify freedom, sexuality, power, ambition, spirituality, transition and strength in groups. In Greek myth, Pegasus, the winged horse, was born from the blood of the snake-haired goddess Medusa. In Celtic myth, white horses are associated with the goddesses Rhiannon and Epona. In Greek mythology, a centaur is half man and half horse. The centaur Chiron was rejected at birth by his human mother, but later became a great compassionate healer. In medical studies, horses have been recognized for their healing effect on humans.

ELEPHANT

There are two species of elephants: the African and the Asian. The word 'elephant' has its origins in the Greek word meaning 'ivory'. Elephants are the largest land animals, with the largest brains. They are capable of expressing grief, using tools, showing compassion and demonstrating self-awareness. Because of their abilities, elephants are a symbol of wisdom in Asian cultures, where they are admired for their memory and high intelligence. Aristotle praised elephants as the animal that surpassed all others in wit and mind.

DEER

Known for its endurance, grace and long life, the deer is a Chinese symbol for longevity. In Palaeolithic cave paintings at Trois-Frères in France, the figure of a shaman known as The Sorcerer wears antlers embodying the deer-spirit. Many ancient cultures identified the deer with rebirth, because it annually sheds and regrows its antlers. Stags were associated with Cernunnos, the Celtic horned god of nature and hunting. Deer are represented in heraldry by the stag or hart.

LEOPARD

The leopard is an agile and stealthy predator. Known as one of the most capricious of the big cats, it is fitting that it draws the chariot of the wine-loving Greek god Dionysus. A ubiquitous African symbol of royal power, the leopard appears on the coats of arms of several African nations, including Benin, Malawi, Somalia and the Democratic Republic of the Congo. Because it is the only cat known to hunt for pleasure rather than hunger, the leopard symbolizes the dangers and dark side of power.

LION

Although dangerous to humans in the wild, lions are considered strong but gentle. Often called the King of Beasts, the lion is a popular symbol of royalty. One of the key animals in heraldry, it is associated with courage, majesty and prowess. Mark the Evangelist, the author of the second Gospel, is symbolized by a lion. Although lions are not native to China, the Chinese celebrate the New Year with the Lion Dance to scare away demons and ghosts. In ancient Egypt, the goddess Sekhmet was depicted as a fierce lioness.

WOLF

Human traits assigned to wolves include intelligence, cunning, sociability and compassion. In the Christian tradition, the wolf represents the devil as the spoiler of the flock. In Roman mythology, a she-wolf suckled Romulus and Remus, the founders of Rome. The wolf was sacred to Mars, god of war. In Japan, grain farmers once worshipped wolves by leaving food offerings near their dens, praying to them to protect their crops from wild boars and deer. For the Aztecs, a howling wolf symbolized Xochipilli, god of dance.

TIGER

In eastern Asia, the tiger represents royalty, fearlessness and wrath. Its forehead markings resemble the Chinese character for 'king'. In imperial China, a tiger symbolized war and represented the highest-ranking general. The Chinese god of wealth, Tsai Shen Yeh, rides a ferocious tiger to guard his money chests. The Hindu goddess Durga also rides a tigress into battle. In Buddhism, the tiger symbolizes unconditional confidence, disciplined awareness, kindness and modesty. Relaxed yet energized, it represents the state of enlightenment.

COYOTE

The coyote is revered and feared by Native Americans. It can provide the knowledge and tools for survival, but is also volatile and unreliable. It is a shape-shifter, a trickster and a transformer. For Native Americans, the coyote is important as a mythological creature rather than as a real animal, and represents the First People, a mythic race who populated the world before humans. They had superpowers and created everything in the world, but were, like humans, capable of both bravery and cowardice, wisdom and stupidity.

FOX

As an animal that roams at the transition times of dawn and dusk, the fox represents shape-shifting and the faery realms. Foxes charm their prey by twirling around and acting stupidly, until the animal draws within striking distance. Because of their method of hunting, foxes came to be known for their slyness and cunning. The Japanese revered them as the divine messengers of Uka no Mitama, the Shinto rice goddess. Because of their craftiness, beauty and solitary nature, foxes appeared frequently in Aesop's Fables.

JACKAL

Anubis, the ancient Egyptian god of embalming and the underworld, was depicted as a man with a jackal's head. The jackal, whose opportunistic diet includes carrion, can find a dead body in the open desert, as Anubis guides the dead along their journey in the pathless underworld. The Hindu goddess Durga is often linked with the jackal. The name of Shiva means 'jackal' as he is the consort of Kali , the destroyer aspect of the Great Goddess. The jackal is also known as a trickster.

BEAR

The bear represents strength, cunning and ferocity in protection of its family, the bear is also a favourite animal on coats of arms. Bears are associated with crystals that are found deep in the caves where they hibernate. Crystals heal through resonance and vibration and by means of the realignment of subtle energies. The bear, the largest of carnivores, is associated with the goddess Artemis/Diana and with the lunar cycle. The Berserkers were ancient Nordic warriors who wore bear shirts into battle, hoping to embody the bear's immense fighting abilities.

MONKEY

One of the most popular Hindu deities is Hanuman, the monkey god known for his courage, perseverance, selflessness and devotion. In the Chinese zodiac, people born in the year of the monkey are often inventors, entertainers and the creative geniuses behind any undertaking. In general, the monkey symbolizes intelligence and the ability to solve problems. Today, capuchin monkeys are being trained from birth as service animals for those with serious spinal injuries, performing tasks such as opening bottles and putting food in a microwave.

BABOON

The baboon had several manifestations in Egyptian mythology. The baboon god Baba was worshipped in pre-dynastic times and may be the origin of the animal's name. The baboon was also considered sacred as one of the manifestations of Thoth, the god of writing and 'one who thinks well'. It was considered a protector, inspirer and an important guide of the writing profession. The baboon was also a magician and skilled at reading all sorts of signs. Not surprisingly, a team of psychologists has recently found evidence of abstract thought in baboons.

BADGER

When defending its home, the badger is remarkably fierce and protective. Because it symbolizes bravery and courage under attack, it is used widely on European coats of arms. Its skill at digging has led to folk beliefs that its paws offer good luck in childbirth. The Pueblo Native Americans consider the badger to be a great healer. Other Native Americans tribes revere it as a storyteller and a keeper of history, legend and lore. The badger is the power animal of medicine women and the keeper of medicinal roots.

BEAVER

Capa the beaver is an animistic spirit of the Lakota tribe. He is regarded as the patron of hard work and domestic tranquillity. In European heraldry, the beaver represents protection and dedication. It is also known for its industry and perseverance, vigilance and self-sacrifice, and is an emblem of cooperation and community. In Christianity, the beaver symbolizes chastity and sacrifice. The American beaver is the national animal of Canada and is depicted on the Canadian five cent piece; it also featured on the first postage stamp issued in the Canadian colonies in 1849.

MOUSE

In ancient Greece and Rome, mice symbolized negative qualities such as avarice, greed and thievery because of their destruction of grain stores. In Hindu lore, the deity Ganesha rides a mouse, as a symbol of intelligence and the ability to penetrate all obstacles. In many cultures the human soul is thought to leave the body in the shape of a mouse at death or while dreaming. In Africa, diviners use mice to determine fortunes. Because mice live so near the ground, they are believed to have a close relationship with earth spirits and ancestors.

RAT

The rat is associated with aggression, death, war, plague and pestilence. However, the attributes of the Chinese astrological sign of the rat are overwhelmingly positive. Rats are viewed as industrious and clever and the Year of the Rat is considered one of fortune and prosperity. For Hindus, the rat represents prudence and foresight, because rats can be seen leaving a ship before it sinks. To the ancient Egyptians, rats symbolized wisdom. In Japan, a white rat is the symbol of Daikoku, the god of prosperity.

BAT

The bat represents rebirth, transition and initiation, and night is the bat's time of power. The bat is sacred in Tonga, West Africa, Australia and Bosnia, and it is often considered the physical manifestation of a soul. It was also sacred to the Aztec, Toltec and Mayan people as a symbol of rebirth and initiation. In China, the bat was associated with Show-Hsing, the god of longevity. In folklore, bats are closely associated with vampires, who are said to be able to transform themselves into bats. Among some Native Americans, the bat is a trickster spirit. In Poland and Macedonia, the bat is a symbol of good luck. In Japan, the bat symbolizes chaos, unrest and unhappiness. In Native American cultures, the bat is often the totem of the shaman, who teaches people to go into the night of inner darkness and emerge reborn.

Insects

Insects have many symbolic meanings, their behaviour suggesting human virtues such as tenacity, patience and adaptability. One of the first-known insect gods was the scarab beetle worshipped as Khepri, the Egyptian god of the sun.

BUTTERFLY

The fragile, short-lived butterfly symbolizes human frailty and the ephemeral nature of life. For Christians, the stages of caterpillar, pupa and winged adult symbolize spiritual transformation. For the Aztec and Maya, the butterfly was the symbol of the god of fire, Xiutecuhtli, as fire transforms both food and metal. For Canadian native tribes, the butterfly is associated with the trickster because of its unpredictable flight.

MOTH

The nocturnal moth symbolizes dreams, otherworldliness and psychic awareness. It is a symbol of the soul yearning for the divine and consumed by mystical love, as the moth is attracted to the candle flame and burns its wings. On a mundane level, a moth burning its wings may be seen as a symbol of frivolity and stupidity. The moth can also represent the human condition, as stated in the Sanskrit text, the Bhagavad Gita: 'Men rush to their doom like moths flying to their death in the candle flame.'

DRAGONFLY

In old Europe, the dragonfly was seen as sinister and was linked to evil and misfortune. In Swedish folk tales, dragonflies were used by the devil to weigh people's souls. The Norwegians called them 'eye pokers', while the Dutch called them 'horse biters'. On the other hand, for Native Americans dragonflies represent the positive qualities of swiftness and activity. They are said to symbolize renewal after periods of hardship. In Japan, dragonflies are symbols of courage, strength and happiness. The Vietnamese forecast rain by the height at which dragonflies fly.

FLY

In mythology, flies represent evil, death and decay – as in the fourth of the ten plagues of Egypt in the Bible. Or they represent nuisances – as when the Greek god Myiagros was charged with chasing flies away during sacrifices to Zeus and Athena. In some fables, like the one about the fly on the coach wheel, the fly symbolizes an ineffectual and annoying person. However, in the traditional Navajo religion, Big Fly is an important spirit being, who acts as a mentor and advice-giver, especially to men.

CICADA

For Buddhists, the cicada symbolizes rebirth, as humans shed their bodies the way cicadas shed their skin. Because the ancient Chinese observed cicadas emerge from full-grown but seemingly dead nymphs, they placed cicada-shaped funeral jades on the tongues of the dead to ensure immortality. The cicada symbolizes the Greek god Tithonus, lover of Eos, goddess of the dawn, who asked Zeus to make Tithonus immortal, but forgot to request that he remain youthful. He lived for ever, but became so old that he was transformed into a cicada.

CRICKET

In ancient Chinese culture, crickets were appreciated for their singing, their vitality and their fascinating life cycles. Because crickets are able to lay hundreds of eggs, people would bless their friends to have as many children as the cricket. But because most crickets sing in the autumn and die with the coming of winter, in poetry they were a symbol of loneliness, sadness and sympathy for the fate of all humans. Crickets were kept in small cages as symbols of good luck and virtue, near windows so that their song could be enjoyed at night.

LOCUST

A devouring swarm of locusts represents a destructive scourge or a hellish invasion. Locusts can symbolize spiritual, psychological or moral torment, or hell-born torments requiring exorcism. In Exodus, one of the plagues of Egypt was a swarm of locusts. In agriculturally rich Egypt, people wore amulets inscribed with the image of a locust to ward off destructive swarms and they also used the locust as a metaphor. On a wall in the temple near modern-day Luxor an inscription reads: 'Battalions will come like the locusts.'

BEE

In many cultures bees have been thought of as messengers of the spirits. In Celtic lore they represent the wisdom of the other world. In the ancient world, bees represented the soul and, when carved on tombs, symbolized immortality. On ancient coins from the city of Ephesus, a queen bee appears as a symbol of the Great Mother. The Roman god of love, Cupid, is often pictured with bees or being stung. During the medieval period monasteries were centres of bee-keeping and so in Christianity the bee came to symbolize industry, fidelity and virginity.

ANT

Ants symbolize strength, hard work and supportive social structures. Fables and children's stories, such as Aesop's *The Grasshopper and the Ant*, represent industriousness and cooperative effort. In the Book of Proverbs in the Bible, humans are exhorted to emulate ants. In some African cultures, ants are considered to be messengers of the gods. In Native American Hopi mythology, they are believed to be the first animals. The Japanese word for ant, *ari*, is represented by the character for insect combined with the character that signifies moral rectitude, propriety.

BEETLE

The dung beetle, often referred to as the scarab, was sacred to ancient Egyptians. In wall paintings, it pushed the sun along its course in the sky, just as the dung beetle rolls balls of dung to its nest. For Taoists, the scarab's dung ball represented the sacred work necessary to achieve immortality. In South American native mythology, a big scarab beetle named Aksak modelled man and woman from clay. The stag beetle was associated by German artist Albrecht Dürer (1471–1528) with Christ in various paintings.

SCORPION

Scorpions symbolize transitions, death and dying, sex, control, treachery and protection. In the ancient Sumerian poem, the *Epic of Gilgamesh*, Gilgamesh sets out to descend to the Land of the Dead. On the way he passes the two mountains from where the sun rises, which are guarded by scorpion folk. In Greco-Roman mythology, Artemis engaged the celestial scorpion to sting Orion's foot, causing his death. Scorpio is the eighth sign in the Western zodiac. In the Christian tradition, a scorpion symbolizes Judas Iscariot, the epitome of treachery.

SPIDER

The spider represents resourcefulness, mystery, power, growth, the feminine, death, rebirth and fate. Most spiders have eight eyes and all have eight legs. The number eight on its side is a lemniscate, or a symbol of infinity. In Greek mythology, Arachne was a gifted weaver but arrogant, and she challenged Athena to a weaving duel. Insulted by the image of Zeus's loves that Arachne wove, the goddess punished her and Arachne killed herself. In remorse, Athena resurrected Arachne in the form of a spider so that she would for ever be the best weaver of the universe.

Birds

From ancient times, in many cultures, birds have functioned as gods, oracles and messengers. Because of their swift flight and sudden appearance, they are often read as omens of good or ill. Their domain is the air element, so they are frequently considered to be mediators between the earthly and heavenly realms – or the physical and spiritual worlds. As humans observed the flight of birds, it was easy to see them as a symbol of the human soul. In Christianity, birds often signify the presence of God, as in the dove symbolizing the Holy Spirit or the sparrow representing God's concern for the most insignificant living things.

GOOSE

The goose symbolizes migrations and transitions, as well as the hearth and home, as it returns to the same spot every spring. In China and ancient Egypt, geese were regarded as messengers between heaven and earth. When a new pharaoh was proclaimed, four geese were sent out in four directions to announce his arrival. In ancient Rome, geese were kept as guardians of the temple of Juno and would cackle loudly when strangers approached. In the Celtic tradition, geese were messengers from the otherworld and it was forbidden to use them as food.

DUCK

In cultures around the world, the duck attracts much humour and silliness and has inspired many cartoon characters. Because it floats on the surface of the water, the duck symbolizes superficiality, chatter and deceit. However, the duck can also dive underwater and reappear in a very different location – in colloquial language it has 'ducked out'. Ducks also symbolize gracefulness and friendliness. In Chinese and Japanese culture, a Mandarin duck and drake pictured together represent marital happiness and fidelity. Ancient Egyptians associated the duck with marshland, a mysterious, dangerous, yet life-giving place.

HEN

The hen symbolizes self-sacrifice, nurturing, protection and comfort. In the 1st century CE the Roman historian Plutarch praised the hen as using all parts of her body to cherish her chicks – letting down her wings and arching her back for them to climb on. In the Bible, Jesus uses the hen and her sheltering wings to describe Christian love as being like a mother's love for her children. In the Congo, the hen serves as the conductor of the soul in the initiatory rites of female shamans of the Bantu tribes.

COCK

In most cultures, the cock is a solar symbol and a sign of illumination. In the Christian tradition, the cock crowing was said to wake men and women out of their secular sleep into the spiritual world of the Gospel. Cock weathervanes on churches symbolized vigilance against evil. When the cock crowed at dawn, all evil things of the night – ghosts, vampires and evil spirits – were said to vanish. Because it shares its food with the hen, the cock symbolizes generosity. Because of its bravery, it is associated with the Greek god Ares.

STORK

Because storks are deeply devoted to their offspring, they are symbols of good parenting. For early Christians the stork represented a respected marriage of virgins, but although mistakenly thought to mate for life, in reality storks practise serial monogamy. In rural Denmark, a stork building a nest on a roof means bad luck and suggests that a death will occur in the house within a year. In Bulgarian folklore, the sighting of a stork returning from its winter migration is a sign of spring. Sometimes Western parents tell young children that 'a stork brought the baby.'

SWAN

The Celts wore images of pairs of swans around their necks for protection. In Hindu culture, the swan signifies the mind of God and a swan is the mount of the goddess Saraswati. In *The Ugly Duckling* fable by Hans Christian Andersen, a mistreated ugly duckling (in reality a cygnet) grows up to be a breathtakingly beautiful swan. Because swans mate for life, they symbolize love, trust and fidelity. In the Greek mythology of Leda and the swan, Helen of Troy was born of the union of Zeus (disguised as a seductive swan) and Leda, a Spartan queen.

DOVE

The moaning call of the dove is associated with sex and childbirth, but the dove is also a symbol of purity and peace. In the Old Testament, Noah sent out a dove to see if the waters had receded and it returned with an olive branch, signifying a truce between God and humans. A dove, as a symbol of a pure soul, is depicted flying from the mouth of martyred Christian saints. When John the Baptist baptized Christ, he saw the Holy Spirit descend like a dove upon him.

LARK

The lark, or skylark, symbolizes the marriage of heaven and earth as it flies swiftly upwards and then dives back down to the ground. Its early morning song and flight symbolize youthful enthusiasm, merriment and the human desire for happiness. It is also the symbol for hope, happiness, good fortune and creativity. For Christian mystics, the lark's song symbolized a joyful prayer to God. Shakespeare twice refers to the lark 'singing at heaven's gate.' In Romeo and Juliet, the lark symbolizes daybreak.

PEACOCK

The peacock is a favourite bird on many coats of arms, symbolic of personal pride. It is also the bird of the Hindu god Krishna who wears peacock feathers in his hair, and it is associated with the Japanese and Chinese goddesses of mercy, Kannon and Kwan Yin. In Buddhism, the peacock's ability to eat poisonous snakes is a symbol of the transmutation of evil into good. In Islam, peacocks are said to be the greeters at the gates of paradise. In the Christian tradition, the peacock is a symbol of eternity and immortality.

EAGLE

The eagle's wings symbolize protection, and the gripping talons and sharp beak represent the threat of destruction. Many nations and organizations use the eagle on their coats of arms. In Christianity, the eagle symbolizes John the Apostle and its soaring quality stands for the first chapter of his Gospel. The eagle is a sacred bird to many Native American tribes and eagle feathers are central to numerous religious customs and tribal ceremonies. The eagle, as spiritual being and ancestor, sometimes appears on totem poles.

FALCON

The falcon is solar and male, and represents spirit, visionary power, light, freedom, guardianship and victory. It symbolizes the lifting of spirit, intellect and morals. The falcon was associated with the rising sun in Egypt. It represented the Egyptian god Horus, who was shown with the head or body of a falcon. In European mythology, the falcon was a symbol of war and the hunt and was associated with the Germanic sky gods Wodan and Frigg. For Peruvian Incas, the falcon symbolized the sun.

OWL

The owl signifies wisdom, intelligence, mystery, mysticism and secrets. In ancient cultures it was considered the ruler of the night, guardian of the underworlds and protector of the dead. In ancient Greece, the owl was sacred to the goddess Athena. Because of its ability to see at night, the owl was invoked by Native Americans as an oracle of hidden knowledge. In Europe, during medieval times, owls were considered witches and wizards in disguise. In Indian culture, a white owl is a companion of Lakshmi, the goddess of prosperity.

RAVEN

In some later Western European traditions, ravens symbolize ill omens, misfortune and death. In contrast, many indigenous people of North America and north-east Asia revere the raven as a god. In China and Japan, the raven symbolizes filial gratitude and family affection. The raven was also associated in China with the sun. In ancient Greece, the raven was a bird sacred to Apollo, where it acted as a messenger to the gods. For the Likuba tribe of the Congo Basin, the raven provided a warning of dangers.

PARROT

In world mythology, because of their talkativeness, parrots are the messengers between humans and gods. In Indian mythology, the chariot of Kama, god of love, is drawn by a parrot. The parrot is also an emblem for Devi and other female deities. In the European Christian tradition, the parrot was a symbol of the Immaculate Conception, which was considered to have taken place in an exotic country – the bird talking into Mary's ear stood for the Conception taking place through the ear, via the Word of God.

OSTRICH

In mythology, the ostrich is said to hide its head in the sand at the first sign of danger. From this derived the old saying 'Don't hide your head in the sand', meaning that one should not ignore a problem, hoping it will go away. Ancient naturalists, noting that the ostrich would eat anything, thought it ate iron and because of this misconception the ostrich is shown in heraldry with a horseshoe in its mouth. In the Book of Job in the Bible, the ostrich also symbolizes a neglectful parent.

PELICAN

During the nesting season some pelicans grow red feathers on their breast and as a result, in medieval Europe, the female pelican was believed to wound her breast with her long, curved bill, drawing blood to feed her young. Because of this misunderstanding, the pelican became a symbol of self-sacrifice and maternal love. The pelican also became a symbol of the Passion of Jesus Christ and the Eucharist. The emblems of the two Corpus Christi colleges, one at Oxford and the other at Cambridge, is a pelican (*corpus christi* means 'Body of Christ'). In heraldry, the pelican is always shown 'wounding' or 'vulning' itself.

Fish, reptiles and amphibians

Symbol of Christianity and Christ, the fish was linked by the pagan cultures of northern Europe to fertility and feminine power. In Indian cultures, it was linked with reincarnation and life force. In ancient Greece, 'fish' and 'womb' were synonymous and the *esica piscis* (a pointed oval) referred to the Great Mother.

Reptiles and amphibians symbolize cycles, change, duality and mystery: the snake sheds its skin, the tadpole transforms into a frog and amphibians are able to exist in two worlds or two environments. In ancient Egyptian and Greek symbolism, the reptile represented divine wisdom and good fortune and was an attribute of Hermes. In Roman mythology, the reptile, which was thought to sleep through the winter, symbolized death and resurrection. Early Christianity associated the lizard with the devil, yet the Polynesians and Maoris it as a god. In India, *nagas* are semi-divine beings with serpent bodies.

CARP

As the carp swims upstream, the Japanese associate it with perseverance in adversity. The carp, or koi, stands for courage and worldly aspiration and achievement. On Children's Day, the Japanese display carp-shaped kites and windsocks to summon strength and success for their offspring. In Chinese art and literature, a jumping carp symbolizes a leap in social status through promotion or marriage.

SALMON

Irish hero Fionn mac Cumhaill gains his powers of perception from eating the 'salmon of knowledge'. In Welsh myth, the salmon is the world's oldest animal. In Norse mythology, the trickster god Loki turns into a salmon to escape punishment from the other gods. For Native Americans, the salmon symbolizes rebirth and renewal. As the salmon dies after spawning, it is associated with the spirits of the dead.

CONCH

Conch shells are used as musical wind instruments in Hindu culture and some island cultures. The Sanskrit epic, the *Mahabharata*, describes warriors of ancient India blowing conch shells as they go into battle. The Hindu god Vishnu holds a conch shell named Panchjanya that symbolizes life emerging from water. The conch is one of the Eight Auspicious Symbols of Buddhism and symbolizes Buddha's voice preaching the Dharma. It is also a symbol of the Greek god Poseidon and, in Islam, it is the ear that hears the divine Word.

LOBSTER

The lobster, a lunar being, symbolizes cycles, regeneration and protection. It casts off its shell for a new one and thus represents rebirth. Its hard, external skeleton represents personal protection. As a scavenger, the lobster symbolizes the ability to make use of every aspect of experience. In ancient Peru, the Moche people worshipped sea animals and lobsters appeared frequently in their imagery. In Japanese culture, the lobster represents longevity and happy, celebratory events. It is especially associated with New Year.

OCTOPUS

The octopus symbolizes mystery, flexibility, adaptability unpredictability, fluidity and intelligence. It is a lunar creature, affected by the tides and the waxing and waning of the moon. It dwells on the ever-changing bottom of the ocean and, not having a skeleton, can move quickly and escape from the tightest places. It has the capability to detach a limb in order to free itself from a predator. The octopus symbolizes creativity, moving towards goals in unorthodox ways and the ability to lose excess emotional or physical baggage.

DOLPHIN

Since ancient times humans have been attracted to the dolphin's intelligence, graceful body, effortless movement, human-like eyes and permanent 'smile'. In Christianity, because dolphins swam alongside boats, they became a symbol of Christ who guides souls to heaven. In an Inuit legend, a young girl named Sedna refused to marry; when her enraged suitors tried to drown her at sea, she grasped the edge of the boat, but the men chopped off all her fingers. Her severed fingers fell into the ocean and turned into the world's first whales, dolphins, seals and walruses.

WHALE

The whale represents the tomb and regeneration. In the myth of Jonah and the whale, the swallowing of Jonah by the whale symbolizes the 'death' that takes place during spiritual initiation. His ejection from the whale's belly after three days represents the subsequent resurrection and rebirth. In Christianity and some Polynesian myths, passing through the belly of a whale was seen as a descent into hell. In Islamic mythology, God created the whale as a foundation for the cosmos and whenever it moved, it caused earthquakes.

SHARK

The shark is a symbol of the dangers of nature and often represents terror and violence. In Hindu mythology, Vishnu is sometimes portrayed as emerging from the mouth of a shark. Hawaiians believed sharks to be the guardians of the sea and Hawaiian mythology features many shark gods. The best known of these was Kamohoali'i, the brother of the goddess Pele. Ka'ahupahau was a goddess born human with bright-red hair, who was later transformed into a shark in order to protect the people who lived on O'ahu from other sharks.

LIZARD

The lizard symbolizes subtlety, sensitivity, quickness and intuitive and psychic abilities. It recognizes the subtlest movements in others and can remain virtually motionless to mislead its prey or protect itself. Lizards have long tails that lend balance and they can be detached and regrown as needed. In ancient Egypt and Greece, the lizard symbolized divine wisdom and good fortune. In Roman mythology, lizards were thought to sleep through the winter and therefore represented death and resurrection. In some Native American traditions, the lizard is associated with dreamtime and dreams.

CHAMELEON

A chameleon can change skin colour in response to light and temperature, as well as emotions and the presence of a mate. In Christianity, the chameleon symbolizes the devil taking different appearances to deceive and attract humans. Because a chameleon's eyes move independently, chameleon charms and talismans were used in ancient Rome as a cure for blindness. For Sufis, a chameleon symbolized an inconsistent person – one who changed his being to suit the circumstances.

SALAMANDER

Salamanders have a strong symbolic relationship to fire that likely originates from their practice of hibernating in dead and rotting logs. When wood was brought indoors and put on the fire, a salamander magically appeared from the flames. As it exudes a moist, milky substance when frightened, the idea emerged that the salamander could withstand fire. In heraldry, it is depicted surrounded by flames and it became the traditional emblem of the blacksmith. In Christianity, the salamander was a symbol of faith and virtue, which triumphs over the fires of passion.

FROG

In folklore, frogs are powerless and ugly but brimming with undeveloped, hidden talents. Laying many eggs, they symbolize fertility and abundance. In Egypt, Heket is the frog-headed goddess of birthing. In Christianity, the frog's three stages of development – egg, tadpole and adult amphibian – symbolize spiritual evolution. In Christian art, the frog is a symbol of the Holy Trinity. For the Celtic people, it stood for healing. In China, the frog or toad is an emblem of good luck.

ALLIGATOR/CROCODILE

Inhabiting both land and water, alligators and crocodiles (known collectively as crocodilians) represent contradiction and the duality of nature. In ancient Egypt, crocodiles were considered sacred, as well as being feared and reviled. They were also equated with the fertility of the life-giving waters of the Nile. In the city of Crocodopolis, crocodiles were adorned with earrings and fed daily to honour Sobek, the crocodile-headed god. In China, the alligator was thought to have invented singing and the drum. And the *Crocodylus porosus*, an ancient giant crocodile, may be the origin of dragon lore in China. The sensitivity of the crocodile to changes in air pressure and coming rain may have been the source of the dragon's mythical ability to control rain and weather. For Aboriginal Australians, the crocodile is associated with wisdom. In West Africa, the crocodile's liver and entrails are used by shamans to cast maleficent spells.

SNAKE

The snake trying to swallow its tail is a symbol for eternity and life begetting life. One of the most complex symbols in the world, the snake symbolizes male and female, death and destruction, life and resurrection, light and darkness, good and evil, healing and poison, wisdom and blind passion. As it sheds its skin, it represents letting go of the past and rebirth. The snake lives in the underworld, or realm of the dead, and represents both the unconscious and transcendence. As a phallic symbol, it represents sexuality and sexual union.

TORTOISE

The tortoise, as representative of the lunar, feminine principle, symbolizes water, the moon, earth goddesses, creation, fecundity and immortality. In creation myths it is often depicted as holding up the world. For Taoists, the tortoise symbolized the whole universe: its shell stood for the heavens; its body, for humans; its flat base, for the earth. Like the crane, the tortoise is a symbol of longevity. For Hindus, it is an emblem of Vishnu, the preserver. For the Japanese, it was a companion of the river goddess Benten, patron of the arts.

Mythical creatures

These chimerical creatures are composites of different parts of different beasts, such as the head of one animal and the torso of another, with magical attributes such as dragon wings. Fantastical beasts symbolized the chaos of the real world, where a life could be altered in the blink of an eye. Winged, clawed monsters were popular in heraldry, where they protected the charge.

DRAGON

Dragons appear all over the world, the European and Oriental dragons being the two most familiar examples. Reptilian monsters all possess magical or spiritual qualities. In Eastern cultures, dragons are beneficent and symbolize nature's primal forces, supernatural power, wisdom and strength. In the West, they are often destructive and evil, representing monsters that a hero must fight. They can be male or female and often guard land, portals or treasures.

WYVERN

A wyvern is a legendary two-legged winged dragon with a serpent's tail, often found in medieval European heraldry. Wyverns symbolize strength, valour, protection and vision, especially in their role as guardians of clan members and treasure. They also represent power and endurance. The wyvern was associated with the rulers of Wessex in South and South West England.

CHIMERA

The chimera is a hybrid monster with a lion's head and legs, a goat's body and a snake's or dragon's tail. It may also be shown with three heads, those of a lion, goat and dragon or snake. The lion's head represents a damaging tendency to dominate. The goat's body represents sexual perversion and promiscuity that harms the body. The snake or dragon's tail symbolizes boastful pride contaminating the spirit. The Greek hero Bellerophon defeated the chimera with the aid of his winged horse, Pegasus. A chimera stands for psychological suffering born of unrestrained imagination.

GRIFFIN

The griffin is a masculine creature with the head, wings and talons of an eagle and the body of a lion. It first appeared in 2000 BCE in Asia, then later in Greece, where it was sacred to Apollo and represented solar wisdom and power. In the Middle Ages in Europe, it represented Christ's dual nature as man and god. In heraldry, a griffin symbolizes the bearer having the dual strength of the lion and the eagle. A griffin borne on a shield was said to instil fear in the horses of the bearer's opponents.

HIPPOGRIFF

The hippogriff is a legendary creature, born of a griffin and a mare. It has the head, wings and front legs of a griffin and the hind parts of a horse. This mating was rare, because the griffin considers the horse as prey and so the hippogriff was a symbol of impossible things and unrealizable love. A popular saying in the Middle Ages to express the impossible was 'to cross griffins with horses'. The hippogriff, being easier to tame than a griffin, became the mount for knights in Charlemagne's legends.

SATYR

Male companions of the Greek god Dionysus and the Roman god Bacchus, satyrs symbolized the sex drive and were often portrayed with an erection. In the Greek tradition they appear with a horse's tail. In the Roman tradition they are frequently described as having the upper half of a man and the lower half of a goat. Satyrs are rogues. They are also subversive, shy and cowardly, and love wine, women and boys. They enjoy music and dancing with the nymphs.

CENTAUR

In Greek mythology, the centaur Chiron had the upper body of a man and the lower body of a horse. He was a positive figure, gentle and wise. He was tutored by Apollo and Artemis and in turn was a mentor to others. Rejected at birth by his human mother, he later became a great compassionate healer. Chiron symbolizes suffering as part of the human condition, and the fact that personal knowledge and the experience of suffering can be useful in helping others who are in pain.

UNICORN

A mythological horse with a lion's tail and the hooves of an antelope, the unicorn is often depicted as white in colour with a single horn on its forehead and described as mysteriously beautiful. Its horn was believed to be a powerful antidote against poison. Unlike most mythical creatures, it is good, selfless, magical, pure and innocent. According to legend, only a virgin could capture a unicorn; it would sense her purity and lay its head in her lap. In Christian iconography, the unicorn symbolizes the Incarnation of Christ as well as chaste love and faithful marriage.

SPHINX

A sphinx has the body of a lion and the head of a human. Similar creatures appear in Egypt, Greece and South and South East Asia. In Egypt, the recumbent sphinx guarded the temple or royal tombs – the largest and most famous being the Great Sphinx of Giza. In Greek mythology, the sphinx was a female demon of destruction and bad luck, depicted as a winged lion in a seated position, with a woman's head. She guarded the entrance to the city of Thebes and asked a riddle of travellers who wished to obtain passage.

MANTICORE

The manticore has the body of a red lion, the face and ears of a human and a trumpet-like voice. The mouth contains three rows of teeth and the manticore can shoot out poisoned spines from its tail, paralysing or killing its victims. The manticore myth originated in Persia, where its name meant 'man-eater'. The creature enjoyed attacking humans and would challenge them with riddles before killing them. In the Middle Ages the manticore became the symbol of tyranny, disparagement and evil.

HARPY

In Greek mythology, the harpies were winged female death-spirits known for stealing food from Phineas, a king of Thrace who had the gift of prophecy. Because Phineas revealed too much, Zeus punished him by having the harpies steal the food out of his hands before he could eat. Jason and the Argonauts rescued Phineas by driving off the harpies. The harpies also abducted people and tortured them on the way to Tartarus. They were vicious, cruel and violent and may have been the personifications of the destructive nature of wind.

PHOENIX

The phoenix, a symbol of fire, divinity and invincibility, is a mythical bird with a tail of beautiful gold and red feathers. The symbol is found in many cultures. When the phoenix has lived for 1,000 years, it builds itself a nest of cinnamon twigs in an oak or palm tree and ignites it with the help of the sun. The phoenix and its nest then burn furiously and are reduced to ashes, from which a new, young phoenix arises. It is said that the new phoenix can regenerate itself when hurt or wounded. In Christian art, the phoenix is a symbol of Christ's resurrection.

BASILISK

The mythological basilisk has the head of a bird and the body of a serpent. It symbolizes lust, disease and treachery. It has poisonous breath and can kill with a look. In Christian art, it represents the Antichrist or a manifestation of the devil. To Protestants, the basilisk was a symbol of the papacy. Its origin may be the horned or hooded cobra from India. By the Middle Ages, overactive imaginations had made it a snake with the head of a cock. Chaucer wrote of a basilisk in his Canterbury Tales.

MERMAID

The mermaid is a mythical aquatic creature with the head and torso of a human female and the tail of an aquatic mammal. The mermaid appears in the folk tales of many cultures throughout the world: the water goddess Mami Wata of West Africa; the merrow of Scotland and Ireland; the *rusalkas* of Russia; the naiads of Greece. Mermaids may be characterized as seductive, dangerous or helpful. In Hans Christian Andersen's famous fairy tale, *The Little Mermaid*, the mermaid is told that she can only obtain an immortal soul by marrying a human being.

PLANTS

In earliest times, human beings relied on plants for their survival. The plant world offered hunter-gatherers a multitude of fruits, leaves, flowers and roots for food and medicine. Trees also provided wood for making tools, shelters and fire. With such heavy reliance on their environment, it is not surprising that early humans regarded every aspect of their environment as being alive. Every rock and tree was home to a spirit that had to be propitiated. In a storm, with trees bending and swaying wildly, it was not a big leap to imagine that, like the sky gods, the spirits of the trees were unhappy.

Trees

Connections between gods and trees were common in classical times. The Greek god Apollo was associated with the laurel, the Egyptian god Osiris with the cedar and the Greek goddess Athena with olive trees. At Saturnalia, Romans decorated trees with candles and brought evergreens into their homes to honour the tree spirits and the new year. In the Celtic tradition, trees were venerated as a link between heaven and earth. In Scandinavia, the ash tree, known as Yggdrasil, was a symbol of universal life, connecting Midgard (the dwelling place of humans), Asgard (the home of the gods) and Hel (the underworld). Today, belief in the mystical power of trees continues.

OLIVE

The Roman poet Horace (65–8 BCE) mentions the olive as the main part of his simple diet. In his time, olives were considered to be one of the most perfect foods. The olive leaf was a symbol of abundance, glory and peace, as well as of benediction and purification. It was ritually offered to deities and kings and to the victors of athletic games. The oil from the olive, which was considered sacred, was used in religious ceremonies, burned in lamps in the temples and used to fuel the 'eternal flame' of the original Olympic Games. The olive tree was said to be sacred to the Greek goddess Athena and was her gift to the people of Greece. In gratitude they made her the patron of the city of Athens.

Some olive trees in Italy today are believed to date back to Roman times and several trees in the Garden of Gethsemane in Jerusalem are claimed to date from the time of Jesus. One olive tree in Crete has been verified as being 2,000 years old using tree-ring analysis.

OAK

The oak is a symbol of strength and endurance found in various cultures around the world and is the national tree of many countries, including England, France, Germany, Poland and the United States. Several individual oak trees, such as the Royal Oak in the English West Midlands and the Charter Oak in Connecticut in the US, are of great historical or cultural importance.

In Celtic mythology, the oak represents doors and gateways between worlds or marks the place where portals to the underworld could be erected. In Norse mythology, the oak was sacred to the thunder god, Thor. It is speculated that this was because oaks – being the largest tree in northern Europe – often drew lightning in a storm. In Greek mythology, the oak was a symbol of Zeus and his sacred tree. The oracle of Dodona, in prehistoric north-western Greece, consisted of a holy oak; priestesses and priests interpreted the rustling of its leaves to determine the correct actions to be taken.

There are numerous proverbs about the oak as an inspiration for living, such as 'Mighty oaks from little acorns grow.'

FIG

In the Old Testament, the fig tree was a symbol of prosperity and security. It was from fig trees that Adam and Eve fashioned their first covering. The fig has been used in art throughout the centuries to cover the genitals and as a symbol of chastity. The Bodhi Tree under which the Buddha gained enlightenment is a famous species of fig that is held sacred in India, where it is also a symbol of plenty and immortality. The fig represented spiritual wisdom and ancient Egyptians used the fig in initiation rites.

CEDAR

The cedar tree symbolizes strength and loyalty and is the emblem of Lebanon. It is associated with healing, cleansing and protection. According to the Old Testament, the Temple of Solomon was built of resinous, scented cedar wood and the gum of the cedar was also used for embalming. In Sanskrit, the word for cedar means 'timber of the gods'. Cedar was often found near shrines as it was thought to help reveal the secrets of heaven and drive away malevolent spirits.

HAWTHORN

The hawthorn tree, a sacred tree of Wicca and witchcraft, is associated with Beltane or May Day, the spring celebration that honours the sun god Belenus. In Irish folklore, cutting the hawthorn was considered bad luck because the faeries inhabiting it might be offended. In Germanic lore, the hawthorn is a symbol of death and its wood is used on funeral pyres. In Greece, wedding couples traditionally wore crowns of hawthorn blossom. Cardea, the Roman goddess of marriage and childbirth, was associated with the hawthorn tree.

HAZEL

The hazel tree symbolizes hidden wisdom, dousing and divination. In mythology, the hazel functions as a container of ancient wisdom and eating its nuts is said to bring about heightened spiritual awareness. In the Celtic legend of Fionn mac Cumhaill, he gains wisdom by eating a salmon that fed on hazelnuts. (Interestingly, contemporary scientific studies have shown the hazelnut to be excellent nourishment for brain function.) In Ireland today, a forked hazel branch continues to be used for divining water.

JUNIPER

The juniper tree is associated with warding off illness, negative forces and evil. These trees were burned in ancient Sumeria and Babylonia as a sacrifice to the gods and was sacred to the goddesses Inanna and Ishtar. Fleeing to Egypt with the infant Jesus, Mary and Joseph hid behind a juniper tree to avoid King Herod's soldiers. In Europe, smouldering juniper branches were carried around fields to protect livestock. A female spirit of the juniper tree called Frau Wachholder was called on for retrieving stolen goods.

MAPLE

The maple leaf is the main element of the flag of Canada and is its national emblem. Early North American settlers, who made sugar from the maple, regarded it as a symbol of success and abundance. They would place maple leaves at the foot of the bed to ward off the devil and to encourage the sweetness of conjugal bliss. North American storks use maple branches in their nests, which further associated the tree with love and a new child in the home. In China and Japan, the maple leaf is also an emblem of lovers.

APPLE

In folklore, mythology and religion, apples appear as a mystical or forbidden fruit. God warned Adam and Eve not to eat of the forbidden fruit (thought to be an apple). They did so and were expelled from the Garden of Eden. Thus the apple became a symbol of sexual seduction. It is also emblematic of discord in the Greek story of the golden apple. In return for a golden apple, Paris of Troy was asked to choose the most beautiful of the goddesses. He selected Aphrodite, enraging the other goddesses and indirectly causing the Trojan War.

PINE

The ancient Egyptian people hollowed out the centre of a pine tree and, with the excavated wood, made an image of the tree god Osiris. They then buried the image like a corpse in the hollow of the tree, which was kept for a year and then burned. The pine tree was also associated with the Greek goddess Pitthea and with the wine god Dionysus. Worshippers of Dionysus often carried a cone-tipped wand, because the pine cone was an ancient fertility amulet. For the Romans, the pine tree was worshipped during the spring equinox festival of Cybele and Attis. As an evergreen tree, the pine also symbolized immortality.

Mongolian shamans, or traditional healers, entered pine forests in silence, with reverence for the gods and spirits thought to be living within. In ancient Celtic lands, Druids would light large pine bonfires at the winter solstice to call back the sun. Pine trees were decorated with candles and colourful metallic objects, which gave rise to the tradition of the Christmas tree.

PALM

In ancient Greece and Rome, the palm
branch symbolized triumph and victory.
The palm was sacred to the god Apollo,
who was supposedly born under a palm
tree. The Romans gave palm branches as
rewards for great athletic achievement
or military success. For early Christians,
the palm branch symbolized victory
over sin and darkness. Today, palm
branches are distributed to the faithful
on Palm Sunday, the celebration of the
triumphal entry of Jesus into Jerusalem.

In Judaism, the palm represents peace
and plenty and became a symbol of Judea,
where palm trees grow in abundance.
The palm may also refer to the Tree of
Life in Kabbalah. Muhammad is said
to have built his home out of palm and
the early muezzin may have climbed
a palm to call the faithful to prayer. In
ancient Assyrian mythology, the palm
symbolizes the goddess Ishtar. The
Mesopotamian goddess Inanna was
credited with making dates abundant
and humans fertile. The date palm was
extremely important to the survival of
ancient Near Eastern people because it
provided both food and shade.

Crops and other plants

Many crops and other useful plants have had symbolic meanings. Because of the importance of agriculture to the survival of ancient civilizations, wheat and corn became enshrined in their mythologies and became emblems of their gods and goddesses. In Asia, the ubiquitous bamboo has many meanings. It is a symbol of Eastern culture and is used on a daily basis for building and other practical uses. It also symbolizes grace and strength; its ability to bend in the wind and not break symbolizes resilience and the gentle Way of the Tao. Bamboo's joined stems also symbolize the Buddhist steps to enlightenment.

CORN

Recent genetic evidence suggests that the domestication of corn, or maize, occurred 9,000 years ago in central Mexico. In North American Navajo culture, the female deity Changing Woman (whose name means 'the woman who is transformed time and time again') grows old and becomes young again with the change of the seasons. She also symbolizes the earth and vegetation. For the Navajo, Changing Woman represented corn, reproduction and the fecundity of motherhood.

The Maya and other Mesoamericans considered corn a gift from the gods and cultivating it was a sacred activity. They chose jade, a rare and precious stone, to symbolize corn. According to the sacred book of the Maya, the Popol Vuh, man was created from corn. The discovery of the Maize Mountain, where the corn seeds were hidden, is one of the most popular Mayan tales. In another tale, maize or corn is personified as a woman who is a captured bride. The Huichol people of central Mexico still 'feed' their newly planted corn with blood from a sacred deer.

WHEAT

The oldest surviving example of wheat found to date is from Çatalhöyük, a Neolithic settlement in southern Anatolia, where the wheat that was discovered was 8,500 years old. To early agricultural peoples, wheat sheaves became symbols of a successful harvest, associated with all that is truly nourishing and life-affirming. Wheat was important to the ancient Chinese, who prayed to the god Hou Ji the god of harvests, for a good crop.

In one of the ceremonies of the Eleusinian Mysteries in ancient Greece, a grain of wheat was contemplated in silence. Those taking part in the ritual meditated on the cycles of the seasons and on the miracle of the death of the single seed grain and its subsequent resurrection into a multitude of grains. In this way the participants honoured the goddess Demeter, the fertility goddess who ensured the success of the harvest. In Christianity, St John uses the grain of wheat – which falls on the ground and dies, in order to bring forth much fruit – as a symbol of the resurrection of Christ. In many civilizations, wheat symbolizes the gift of life.

IVY

The clinging aspect of ivy symbolizes true love and faithfulness in marriage and friendship. In Christianity, ivy signifies resurrection and eternal life, as do other evergreens. For medieval Christians who observed that ivy grew on dead trees, it symbolized the immortal soul that survived the dead body. As it thrives in the shade, ivy is associated with debauchery, carousing, sensuality and the enjoyment of forbidden pleasures. The satyrs and Dionysus, the god of wine, often wear wreaths of ivy.

CLOVER

The shamrock, a clover with three leaves, is the symbol chosen by the Irish St Patrick to represent the Holy Trinity. Ancient Celts revered the clover and had many beliefs based on triads, represented in the triskelion, triquetra and triple spiral. The occurrence of threes, as in the clover, was linked to aspects of the Triple Goddess and time's past, present and future. Clover as a food source for livestock stood for abundance and prosperity and its prolific growth represented fecundity. Clover's sweet smell is said to induce calm and contentment.

Bamboo

Bamboo is an ancient plant dating back to the time of the dinosaurs. In China, it represents a strong and resilient character. Because it quickly grows high, straight and strong, the Chinese equate bamboo with straightforward, sincere and spiritual people and with the Way of the Tao. The linked stems of the bamboo also stand for the Buddhist path to enlightenment. An essential element of formal Chinese and Japanese gardens, it is appreciated for its beauty, the soft sound of its leaves in the breeze and the delicate shadows that it casts on garden walls. Bamboo groves are thought to induce calm and stimulate creativity. Bamboo symbolizes the virtues of the ideal scholar: purity, longevity and flexibility. Bamboos provide shade, housing and many ritual and everyday items, including musical instruments, cooking utensils, furniture, baskets, lampshades and hats. There is great reverence and respect for bamboo. The mother bamboo plant with her seedlings all around her symbolizes fertility and the happy family. Bamboo has been a symbol of good fortune in Asian cultures for thousands of years.

Herbs and spices

Herbs and spices have stood as symbols from ancient times. The Greeks bestowed wreaths of bay laurel as a symbol of triumph and peace (the term 'poet laureate' derives from this practice). During the Middle Ages, herbs not only had symbolic meanings but were also believed to have potent magical powers.

PARSLEY

Parsley was placed on graves to please Persephone, who guided the souls of the dead to the underworld. Homer wrote that warriors fed their horses parsley to help them run faster. The Romans wore parsley sprigs in their togas to protect against evil and placed parsley on plates of food against contamination. Botanist William Turner (1508–1568) wrote that parsley thrown in a pond could cure sick fish.

BASIL

Holy basil, or tulsi, is revered in Hinduism and used in the Greek Orthodox Church to prepare holy water. In Europe, basil is placed on the chest of the deceased to ensure a safe journey to heaven. In Africa basil is said to protect against scorpions. In Elizabethan England, guests were given basil to ensure safe passage home. In Italy, a basil plant on a balcony announced that a woman was ready to be courted.

MARJORAM

The Greeks believed that marjoram growing on a grave signalled that the deceased was in a happy place. Both Greeks and Romans crowned young married couples with marjoram. Medicinally, the Greeks used marjoram extensively, both internally for a variety of ailments and externally as a poultice. According to folk medicine, marjoram oil placed in the hollow of an aching tooth relieves pain. Some horse owners use the scent of marjoram oil to calm sexually excited stallions and to sedate horses when transporting them.

MINT

In Greek mythology, Minthe, a naiad, was impressed by Hades' golden chariot. As she was about to be seduced by him, Persephone intervened and metamorphosed her into the sweet-smelling herb of mint. In ancient Greece, mint was used in funerary rites to offset the smell of decay. It was also an ingredient in the fermented barley drink called kykeon, a preparatory psychoactive substance for participants in the Eleusinian Mysteries, which offered the hope of a positive afterlife for initiates. In Central and South America, mint is known as hierbabuena, or the 'good herb'.

ROSEMARY

Symbolizing fidelity and remembrance, rosemary was used as decoration at both weddings and funerals. Anne of Cleves, the fourth wife of Henry VIII of England, wore a rosemary wreath at her wedding and, branches of rosemary, gilded and tied with colourful silken ribbons were presented to wedding guests. In old Europe, sprigs of rosemary were dropped on coffins, symbolizing that the deceased would not be forgotten. Ancient Greek students wore rosemary to enhance their memory during examinations.

SAGE

The ancient Greeks and Romans believed sage imparted wisdom and intelligence. In the 10th-century, Arab physicians associated it with long life. In the 17th century, the English royal family had their servants scatter sage and lavender to hide the stench of the 'great unwashed'. In the Middle Ages, sage was used to treat memory loss, fevers and intestinal problems. First Nations peoples in North America use sage tied in bundles for 'smudging' or purification; the bundle is lit and passed around a room or space to cleanse and purify the area.

THYME

The name thyme comes from the Greek *thymos*, meaning 'spirit'. To the ancient Greeks, thyme restored spirit or vigour. It symbolized graceful elegance, and smelling of thyme was an admirable quality. Roman soldiers bathed in thyme to gain strength and courage for battle. During the Middle Ages, knights wore a sprig of thyme embroidered on their scarves as a sign of their bravery. For ancient Greeks, thyme symbolized sweetness and the honey produced by bees that live near fields of thyme is still considered exceptionally sweet.

GARLIC

Garlic was placed by ancient Greeks on piles of stones at crossroads, as a food offering for the goddess of crossroads, Hecate. A Christian legend relates that when Satan stepped out from the Garden of Eden after the fall of man, garlic sprang up from the spot where he placed his left foot, and an onion from where he placed his right. In many cultures throughout time, garlic was praised for its medicinal uses – especially in warding off infections and in strengthening immunity. It is also thought to be a vampire-repellent.

MISTLETOE

In European folklore, mistletoe is a symbol of fertility and a protection against poison. As an evergreen that produces bright-red berries in midwinter, it symbolized renewal and regeneration. Druids considered mistletoe an aphrodisiac and gathered it from oak trees at the winter solstice. The custom of kissing under mistletoe at Christmas is a survival of this tradition. In the Middle Ages and later on, branches of mistletoe were hung from ceilings to ward off evil spirits and over doors to prevent the entrance of witches.

SAFFRON

Saffron is a spice derived from the stigmas (female parts) of saffron crocus flowers. In the ancient world, the saffron dye and spice obtained from the three female stigmas of each bloom had a value greater than jewels or precious metals, and saffron remains a costly spice today. Saffron was used to dye the garments of women of high status, such as priestesses, in shades from pale yellow to a deep orange-red. In the East, to the present day, saffron-coloured robes are associated with Buddhist and Hindu divinities, as well as with monks and nuns.

Flowers

The symbolic meaning of flowers has varied widely from culture to culture. For example, in 19th-century England the language of flowers was cultivated as a social art. Directories were written to define the meaning of every flower, such as sympathy, love or rejection, and gift bouquets called 'tussie-mussies' were given to convey a secret message to the recipient. In every culture, however, flowers communicate the poignant beauty and brevity of life.

LILY

In present times, lilies are often associated with whiteness and purity of heart, innocence and virginity, and even with heaven and death. Bouquets of white lilies are popular in Christian homes during the Easter holiday as they symbolize Christ's resurrection. The Easter lily, in the shape of a trumpet, heralds the coming of spring. In other Christian traditions, the Madonna lily is considered the special flower of the Holy Virgin Mary.

In Roman mythology, the lily is associated with Venus and the satyrs, its phallic pistil representing procreation. Poets, such as the French poet Stéphane Mallarmé (1842–1898), suggest that lilies are lunar and female, and they are therefore associated with love and sensuality. In medieval times, lilies symbolized feminine sexuality, but afterwards the sensuous lily was perceived through the eyes of repression to become glorious and pure.

In China, the day lily is the emblem of motherhood. The lily also symbolizes harmony and is often given as a wedding gift. Spaniards believed that eating a lily's petals would restore their humanity after they had behaved in a beastly fashion.

ROSE

For the ancient Greeks and Romans, the rose symbolized love and beauty and the goddesses of love – Aphrodite and Venus. Aphrodite gave a rose to her son Eros, the god of love, who in turn gave it to Harpocrates, the god of silence, to ensure that his mother's indiscretions remained secret. In ancient Rome, a rose would be placed on the door of a room where confidential matters were discussed. From this practice derives the phrase sub rosa, or 'under the rose', which means 'to keep a secret'. In the Christian tradition, the phrase sub rosa was associated with confession and roses were often carved on confessionals, indicating that the priest would maintain secrecy.

The red rose eventually became a symbol of the blood of Christian martyrs and of the Virgin Mary. It was also used as a badge by marchers in the May 1968 student protests in Paris and has been adopted as a symbol by various European Socialist parties. The rose is also the national flower of both England and the United States.

DAFFODIL

Today, the daffodil symbolizes spring, rebirth and new beginnings. However, the ancient Greeks associated it with death. Daffodils grew in the meadows where the god Hades captured the goddess Persephone and took her to the underworld. The alternate name for daffodil is narcissus and it is associated with the handsome Greek youth, Narcissus. While walking by a river, he stopped to drink and, taken by his own reflection, he leaned over the water too far, like a drooping daffodil, and drowned.

TULIP

Tulips are associated with Holland, but the flower and its name originated in the Ottoman Empire. They were called *tulipan* after the word *tulbend*, meaning 'turban'. In early 17th-century Europe, 'tulipmania' took hold and the wealthy traded bulbs like stocks and shares. The tulip as a status symbol was then used extensively as a decorative motif in wealthy homes. In early 20th-century America, the tulip became a symbol of hope and post-war wealth, and this prosperous-looking flower is often chosen as a logo for financial institutions.

HYACINTH

In Greek mythology, the hyacinth is associated with the prince Hyacinthus, a beautiful youth loved by the god Apollo. Throwing the discus very hard to impress Hyacinthus, Apollo accidentally killed him and the hyacinth sprang from the blood of the dying prince. Another version states that the wind god Zephyrus was jealous of Hyacinthus's love for Apollo and blew Apollo's discus off course, killing Hyacinthus. When he died, Apollo refused to let Hades claim the boy. Instead, he created the hyacinth flower from the prince's spilled blood.

DAISY

The daisy gets its name from the Anglo-Saxon term *daes eage*, or 'day's eye', referring to the way in which it opens and closes with the sun. Chaucer called it 'eye of the day'. The daisy is associated with childhood innocence, simplicity and modesty. Girls still pluck a daisy's petals one by one, repeating 'He loves me, he loves me not'. When farmers in old England dreamed of daisies in the springtime, they considered it a lucky omen; dreams of daisies in the autumn or winter signalled bad luck.

CARNATION

A red carnation symbolizes passionate and pure love; a pink carnation symbolizes marriage. During the Renaissance, a carnation represented the vow of fidelity and the groom presented the bride with one at the wedding. Rembrandt's portrait *Woman with a Pink* shows a woman holding a pink carnation, symbolizing her marriage to the man in another of his portraits, *Man with a Magnifying Glass*. In Christian legend, Mary wept as she watched Jesus carrying the cross and where her tears fell carnations grew; carnations often appear in paintings of her.

CHRYSANTHEMUM

In ancient China, the chrysanthemum symbolized cheerfulness and rest after the final harvest. Around the 8th century CE the chrysanthemum appeared in Japan and so impressed the emperor that he made it his official crest and seal. For the Japanese, the chrysanthemum is a symbol of the sun and the orderly unfolding of its petals is a symbol of perfection. Japan even has a national chrysanthemum day known as the Festival of Happiness. In Italy, the chrysanthemum is associated with the dead and with funerals.

IRIS

Iris, which in Greek means 'rainbow', gets its name from the Greek goddess of the rainbow, who carried messages from the gods on Mount Olympus to humans. The iris symbolizes royalty and divine protection. The fleur-de-lis, a stylized iris motif, has stood for France and its royalty since the 12th century. During the reign of Louis IX in the 13th century, the three petals of the fleur-de-lis came to represent faith, wisdom and valour, and were said to be a symbol of divine favour bestowed on France. The iris functions as both the national flower and the emblem of France.

MARIGOLD

Marigolds, one of the most widely cultivated flowers in India, are harvested by hand so as not to damage the delicate blooms. Loose marigold blooms or garlands are sold in markets for religious decoration and for offerings. Bright-yellow and orange marigold garlands decorate statues and temples and are offered at funerals, weddings and other ceremonies. Boiling the flowers produces a yellow dye. Old English herbals recommend marigold flowers as a remedy for bee stings, while Mexicans decorate graves with marigolds on the Day of the Dead.

LILAC

Lilacs belong to the genus *Syringa*, the name deriving from the Greek word *syrinx*, meaning a pipe or flute. In Greek mythology, the nymph Syrinx turned herself into a reed to hide from Pan. Pan used the reed to make the first flute. Purple lilacs symbolize first love, while white lilacs embody youthful innocence.

In contemporary Greece, Lebanon and Cyprus, the lilac is strongly associated with Easter because it first blooms around that time. Consequently the lilac there is called *paschalia*. Lilacs are also associated with grief and mourning. In the late 19th century, in Europe and North America, black was worn to symbolize a recent death, but after a year of mourning a widow could change the colour of her clothing to lilac. 'When Lilacs Last in the Door-yard Bloom'd' is an elegy on the death of President Abraham Lincoln (1809–1865), written by the American poet Walt Whitman (1819–1892). Whitman expresses his grief at the loss of Lincoln and grapples with death itself. Like other shades of purple, lilac also symbolizes spirituality.

LOTUS

The lotus is one of the most illustrative symbols of Buddhism. It has its roots in the mud, its stem grows up through the water and the heavily scented flower emerges on top of the water in full sunlight. The lotus, then, becomes the metaphor for the journey of the soul from the primeval mud of suffering, through the waters of spiritual practice, into the bright sunshine of enlightenment. In Buddhism, the human heart is referred to as an unopened lotus, the pristine Buddha nature within waiting to bloom. In many representations of the Buddha he sits on a lotus throne, and numerous Buddhist deities are depicted either sitting on or holding a lotus flower.

The white lotus is associated with the White Tara and proclaims her perfect nature. The pink lotus is linked with the Buddha himself. The red lotus is the lotus of love and compassion and is the flower of Avalokiteshvara, the bodhisattva of compassion. The blue lotus is a symbol of wisdom and an emblem of Manjushri, the bodhisattva of wisdom.

POPPY

In Greek and Roman mythology, poppies were a symbol of both sleep and death. The opium extracted from poppies caused sleep and their blood-red colour stood for death as well as for resurrection from the dead. In these ancient cultures, poppies were used as offerings for the deceased. Today, poppies are carved as decorations on tombstones to symbolize eternal sleep. In Europe, the corn poppy became a symbol of the fallen soldier in the First World War, because it was the only plant that continued to grow in the war-torn fields. On Remembrance Day in Commonwealth countries, and also on Memorial Day in the United States, plastic and paper poppies are worn to remember the veterans of war.

In the East, the drug opium is extracted from the poppy. The drug was known in ancient Greece and Rome and was originally used only as a sedative and for pain relief. Later, in other cultures, it was used as a recreational drug for pleasure. Opium is also one of the most valuable medicinal drugs and morphine and codeine (the two principal alkaloids of the poppy) are extensively used.

ORCHID

The orchid's name derives from the Greek word *orchis*, meaning 'testicle'. In ancient times, Greek women tried to influence the sex of their unborn children with orchid roots. The father would eat large new tubers if a male child was wanted and the mother would eat small tubers if she wanted a female child. The Paphiopedilum orchid was named for Paphos, the temple of the love goddess Aphrodite, located on the island of Cyprus. Perhaps the most famous orchid is the vanilla orchid, the source of vanilla flavouring.

THISTLE

The Scottish thistle, a thorny yet beautiful flowering plant, is an ancient Celtic symbol of pain and suffering, as well as of noble character and birth. King James VII of Scotland (1633–1701) instituted the Order of the Thistle, one of the most ancient British Orders, in 1687. The motto of the Order was *Nemo me impune lacessit* ('No one provokes me with impunity'). In 1262, when the Danes tried to attack Scotland at night, one of the barefoot soldiers yelled in pain as he stepped on a prickly thistle, thus alerting the Scots to the Danish invasion.

AMULETS, CHARMS AND TALISMANS

The words 'amulet', 'charm' and 'talisman' overlap in meaning and are often used interchangeably. Amulets are objects imbued with powers of protection and may be stones, small figures, coins, drawings, pendants, rings, packets of herbs, animal teeth or claws, mirrors or anything else that protects by magical rather than physical means. In Africa, amulets are made of dried animal skins, claws and bark, while in Thailand small figures of the Buddha are worn on chains around the neck. A charm works primarily to attract good luck, health and happiness, while a talisman is imbued with magical powers and often used in ritual, protecting and

Amulets of protection

People wear amulets to protect them from other people, bullets, witches, evil spirits, the devil, vampires and negative energy of all kinds – especially that of the 'evil eye', or the envious gaze of others. Protection is desired for babies and children as well as adults, bicycles and cars, animals and even farm implements. Amulets used for protection are found everywhere in the world and often mix standard religious symbols with folk tales and mythology. In the Islamic world, the hand of Fatima and blue beads are worn to ward off the evil eye. In the West, the crucifix is worn as a declaration of religious faith as well as for protection. The American astronaut Edward White (1930–1967) went into space with a St Christopher's medal in his pocket.

MIDDLE EASTERN HAMSA HAND/HAND OF FATIMA

Many cultures believe that good fortune may attract the jealousy of others who, as a result, will bestow a curse through a malevolent gaze called the 'evil eye'. The hamsa hand is a symbol used in amulets, charms and jewellery to protect against the evil eye. Another name for this amulet is the hand of Fatima, in reference to Fatima Zahra, the daughter of Muhammad. Hamsas are popular in Israel simply as a symbol of good luck. Many Jewish hamsas are decorated with fish or Hebrew prayers.

MIDDLE EASTERN BLUE EYE

A blue eye, also called a nazar or evil-eye stone, is an amulet dating back to ancient mythology that is said to protect against the evil eye. It consists of concentric circles, with dark blue on the outside, then light blue or yellow and finally white with a small dark-blue centre, resembling a blue eye. It is thought that the blue-eye amulet originally derives from the Egyptian Eye of Horus amulet, which is also used for warding off the evil eye. The use of blue-eye amulets is widespread throughout the eastern Mediterranean and the Middle East.

MEXICAN OJO DE DIOS

The Mexican *Ojo de Dios*, or eye of God, is a magical object that symbolizes the power of being able to see what is unknowable. The prayer expressed by the maker is that the all-seeing eye of God will rest upon the supplicant. The *Ojo de Dios* is a weaving usually made of coloured yarn wound around two crossed sticks at right angles. The resultant lozenge shapes create four points representing the elements of earth, fire, air and water. The *Ojo de Dios* is thought to have originated with the Huichol people of Mexico.

ITALIAN HORN

The Italian horn, or *corno*, is an ancient amulet once sacred to the pre-Christian European moon goddess, whose consort was sometimes called the Horned God. A *corno* is a long, gently twisted, horn-shaped amulet worn to protect against the evil eye. It is often carved out of red coral or made of gold or silver. Today the *corno* is found in Italy and in America among descendants of Italian immigrants, and is worn by boys and men to protect their genitalia from the evil eye.

JEWISH LILITH PROTECTION AMULET

In Jewish lore, Lilith was the first wife of Adam, but she refused to be dominated – sexually or otherwise – and abandoned him. She then had erotic encounters with fallen angels and gave birth to an enormous family of demons called the *lilim*. Adam wanted her back, so God sent three angels, Senoy, Sansenoy and Semangelof, to threaten her that if she did not return, 100 of her sons would die every day. She refused, but said that she would seek revenge for the deaths of her children, vowing to kill newborn infants and women in childbirth. However, she agreed that she would not harm any infant or mother wearing an amulet with the images or names of the three angels inscribed upon it.

Lilith amulets are made of silver or paper, or are drawn on the wall as a circle of protection, with the names of the three angels written within. Perhaps because of Lilith's highly sexual nature, women also used her amulet to increase their fertility.

PENNSYLVANIAN HEX SIGNS

The practice of painting hex designs on buildings, as a means of protection against witchcraft, negative rune workings and spells, represents a positive talisman and dates back to the pre-Christian era in Europe. The term 'hex' may derive from the German *Hexe*, meaning 'witch', or from the Greek prefix *hex-*, meaning 'six' – six-sided designs protecting against hexes were common on early Germanic homes and can still be seen above the doors of some buildings. These brightly coloured, geometric designs are today best known as an aspect of the Pennsylvanian Dutch folk art of North America, although the hex signs seen on Dutch barns in central and eastern Pennsylvania are not six-sided and are mostly decorative in nature.

HORSESHOE

The practice of using worn horseshoes as protective talismans originated in Europe, where farmers would nail them above the doors of houses, barns and stables to ward off evil spirits. The crescent shape of the horseshoe evokes the moon and the Greek and Roman moon goddesses Artemis and Diana. The horseshoe represents the Mother Goddess as protectress, symbolizing the fecundity of her sacred vulva and womb, and is also related to other protective doorway goddesses, such as the Irish Sheela-na-Gig, the Roman goddess Cardea and the Blessed Virgin, who is often shown standing on a crescent-shaped moon and placed within a vulva-shaped mandorla (when two circles overlap one another, the space in between forms an almond shape, pointed at both ends, known as the mandorla).

The horseshoe is one of the most common talismans seen in modern North America. If used in its function as a talisman for magical protection, placed over the doorways of barns and stables, the horseshoe is placed with the ends pointing downwards. However, today it is usually placed upwards, in its function as a container or vessel of good luck. In Mexico, used horseshoes are wrapped in colourful thread and sequins, and are sold with holy cards of San Martin Caballero, the horse-rider.

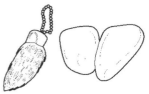

For good luck and prosperity

Good-luck charms come in many different shapes and forms. An example is a rabbit's foot or a four-leafed clover carried on a key chain to bring good luck. In China, crickets in cages are thought to bring good fortune and coins tossed onto the floor are said to bring money. The Japanese maneki neko, which is also called the lucky or beckoning cat, is said to attract customers to businesses when placed beside a cash register.

AMERICAN RABBIT'S FOOT

The rabbit's foot is recognized throughout American culture as a good-luck symbol, but its origin is in the southern, African-American folk-magic tradition. Only the left hind foot of the rabbit was considered lucky and it had to be rubbed in order to bring luck. The auspicious rabbit's foot may be an outgrowth of Br'er Rabbit, the protagonist in the Uncle Remus novels of Joel Chandler Harris (1848–1908), an amalgamation of Cherokee and African trickster-rabbit myths. Today, the rabbit's foot is less popular because of animal-rights issues.

LATIN AMERICAN LODESTONES

A lodestone is a natural magnet. Because of its inherent drawing power, the ancient Romans valued the lodestone as a powerful amulet for increasing power and prosperity. Lodestones are vital in African-American hoodoo (traditional folk magic) practice, and in Latin American budu magic. In Latin America, lodestones are found in packages of amulets for drawing money towards the wearer. The lodestones are sprinkled with magnetic sand or ultra-fine iron shot to enhance their power and may also be rubbed with anointing oil.

JAPANESE MANEKI NEKO

The *maneki neko*, which means 'beckoning cat', is a common Japanese ceramic figurine believed to bring good luck. The sculpture depicts a white cat beckoning with an upright paw and is usually displayed at the entrance of shops and restaurants. The origin of this charm is as follows: one day a samurai passed a cat that seemed to wave at him. Taking the cat's wave as a sign, he went to it and, in doing so, avoided a trap that had been laid for him just ahead. Ever since then cats have been considered lucky spirits.

CHINESE BA GUA MIRROR

The I Ching is a system of yin and yang , which comprises eight trigrams , which in turn form 64 hexagrams. In Chinese, *ba* is the number eight and *gua* means 'trigram', and so the term *ba gua* signifies the eight trigrams. *Ba gua* mirrors are octagonal *ba guas* with mirrors in the centre. They are used to bring harmony and prosperity to a home or office. Ideally, they should be placed near the centre of a room or building. They are also frequently hung above the doors of homes and businesses to bring good luck to all who enter.

CHINESE MONEY TOAD

Chan chu is the name of the lucky money toad, a popular symbol for prosperity that is usually seen in Chinese restaurants and shops. It generally has red eyes and flared nostrils and sits on a pile of money, while holding a coin in its mouth. According to Feng Shui lore, it is believed to protect wealth and increase income. Money toads are placed facing the front door, to invite money in, and are turned backwards at night to prevent the newly earned money from leaving.

JAPANESE DARUMA DOLL

Daruma dolls are hollow, round Japanese wish-dolls with no arms or legs, said to represent Bodhidharma, the founder and first patriarch of Zen. The rounded, weighted doll is painted red, with a face with a moustache, beard and blank white circles for eyes. Using black ink, the owner of the doll fills in the right eye while making a wish. Should the wish later come true, the remaining eye is filled in. Until the wish has been granted, the daruma doll is kept in a high place, often near the Buddhist home altar.

Daruma dolls are usually purchased in or near Buddhist temples. If one was purchased at a particular temple and the wish has not come true, the owner can return it there for burning. Burning usually occurs at the year's end as a purification ritual to let the kami, or spirit within the daruma, know that the owner did not abandon the wish, but will persevere in the next year to make it come true.

For sex and fertility

The human preoccupation with love and sex fuels the continued use of sex amulets and talismans throughout the world. Charms to attract sex and love and to increase fertility have been found in all cultures dating back to antiquity. For example, penis amulets were common in the late Roman era and examples have been found in a spring at an old Roman settlement near York in England. In ancient times, these charms were used as offerings to gods and were tossed into holy wells or springs as a wish for children or for luck in sexual conquests.

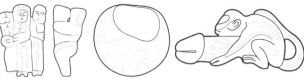

PERUVIAN LOVE CHARMS

The *munachi* is a Peruvian amulet used to cast sexual or love spells. *Munachi* is a Quechua word that combines *muna*, meaning 'to desire' or 'to love', with *chi*, meaning 'to cause to happen'. A *munachi* is a small, simple soapstone carving of a man and a woman engaged in sexual intercourse. A love spell is cast by wrapping a hair from the actual man and woman around the necks of the *munachi* lovers. The *munachi* is then buried in front of the door of the newlyweds' house.

Munaiwarmi means 'woman's love stone' in the Quechua language. The *munaiwarmi* is a small carving depicting a woman holding flowers and a man standing next to her, symbolizing a happy marriage and the potential for children. Quechua women use this amulet to ensure their husbands remain faithful when they are away from home. As with the *munachi*, the *munaiwarmi* is wrapped with a lock of hair from both the man and the woman. The woman may keep it with her or she may give it to her husband to help him resist temptation.

AMERICAN BUCKEYE

In the midwestern United States, men may carry the buckeye in their pockets as a 'lucky piece' to encourage good fortune in sexual encounters. The buckeye – also known as the horse chestnut – is a dark-brown nut with a very shiny, polished skin and a dull, pale-brown scar where it was attached to the inside of the seedpod. The buckeye is so named because it resembles the eye of a buck deer. As a sexual charm, it is a potent symbol, in miniature, of firm, smooth testicles.

THAI PENIS AMULET

The Thai name for a penis amulet is *palad khik*, which means 'honourable surrogate penis'. Boys and men wear these small amulets under their clothes next to their penis to protect it from real or magical injury. The origin of the *palad khik* is the Indian Shiva lingam, which was brought to Thailand by Cambodian monks in around the 8th century CE. The early examples of palad khik are inscribed with praises to Shiva, while contemporary ones feature praises to Buddha. *Palad khik* amulets continue to be made by Thai Buddhist monks.

For healing and thanks

While many amulets and talismans are apotropaic – that is, they ward off evil – charms are meant to attract good luck and prosperity. The milagros and ex votos of Mexico are dedicated to healing: either asking for healing or giving thanks for it to God, Jesus, Mary or one of the saints in the Catholic tradition. The charming and heartfelt paintings known as ex votos traditionally include a handwritten paragraph giving details about the person and the specific difficulty that either requires intervention or has been relieved. They function as visual and written prayers and are hung in the parish church of the supplicant.

MEXICAN MILAGROS

Milagros are small silver or gold votive offerings in the shape of arms, legs, eyes or other body parts, or shaped as animals, fruits or vegetables. They are offered to a favourite saint as a visual symbol of the petitioner's need for healing or in thanks for a prayer answered. Milagros are often attached to statues of saints or to the walls of churches in Mexico. For example, if someone has a broken arm, a tiny silver arm is hung on or near the favourite saint as a prayer for healing.

Milagros can be custom-made by a silversmith or purchased from a vendor outside the church. Their use represents an ancient custom of the Hispanic world, beginning with the Iberians of Spain in the 5th century BCE. Later, milagros accompanied the Spanish into the New World as votive offerings. The use of milagros continues to be an important part of folk culture throughout Mexico, New Mexico, rural areas of Spain and other parts of the Mediterranean.

MEXICAN EX VOTOS

Ex voto is a shortened form of the Latin phrase *ex voto suscepto*, meaning 'from the vow made'. Ex votos are therefore an offering made to a saint or divinity in fulfilment of a vow or simply in gratitude for prayers answered. They can take many forms, but the most famous are small detailed biographical paintings, created on tin or wood, illustrating the circumstances of the supplicant's vow.

Usually executed in a primitive style, the painting may include the person making a vow and the saint or deity petitioned, as well as a paragraph or more of handwritten explanation. For example, the supplicant may promise to give up drinking if their child will be healed or their house will be rid of rats. The text may express this wish, or give thanks for the miraculous healing of the child or the miraculous arrival of a strange cat that exterminated the rats. Ex votos are placed in the church or chapel where the worshipper seeks help or wishes to give thanks.

ALPHABETS AND LETTERS

Western scholars postulate that the first alphabet appeared in Mesopotamia, possibly with the Assyrians whose god Nabu is said to have revealed the cuneiform script to them. Hindus claim that the source of writing lies in India, with the ancient script of the Harappan civilization. And the Chinese assert that it is their written characters that are the oldest on earth. The truth is hidden in antiquity. But for all these ancient cultures, writing – whether used for mundane or religious purposes – was always a divine activity because it was used to convey the mysteries of the gods.

Western magical alphabets

In the West, from the 4th century CE until the 19th century, magical alphabets were created to communicate esoteric and mystical information or for political reasons, enabling indigenous peoples to communicate outside the Roman Latin of their rulers.

ANGELIC ALPHABET

Heinrich Cornelius Agrippa (1486–1535) created the Angelic alphabet during the 16th century for the purpose of communicating with angels. Also known as the Celestial alphabet, it is derived from the Greek and Hebrew languages.

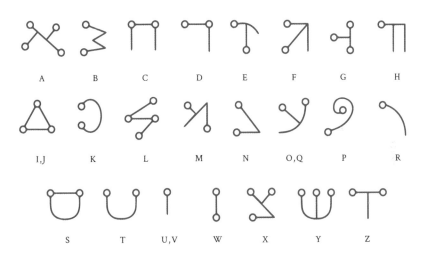

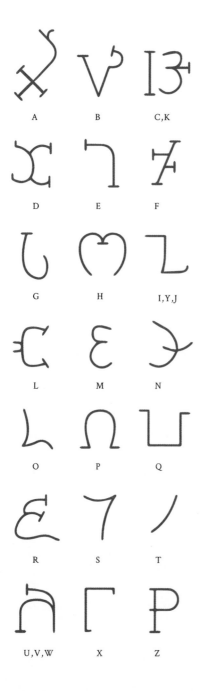

A	B	C,K
D	E	F
G	H	I,Y,J
L	M	N
O	P	Q
R	S	T
U,V,W	X	Z

ENOCHIAN ALPHABET

Dr John Dee (1527–1608), magician and court astrologer to Queen Elizabeth I of England, and his colleague Sir Edward Kelly created this alphabet during the 16th century. Dee and Kelly claimed that angels gave them the alphabet and the Enochian language. Enochian magic was involved in the practice of invoking angels and was also central to the late 19th- and early 20th-century Hermetic Order of the Golden Dawn system of magic that was espoused by Aleister Crowley.

Malachim Alphabet

The Malachim alphabet is derived from the Hebrew and Greek alphabets and was created by Heinrich Cornelius Agrippa during the 16th century. It is still used occasionally by Freemasons today.

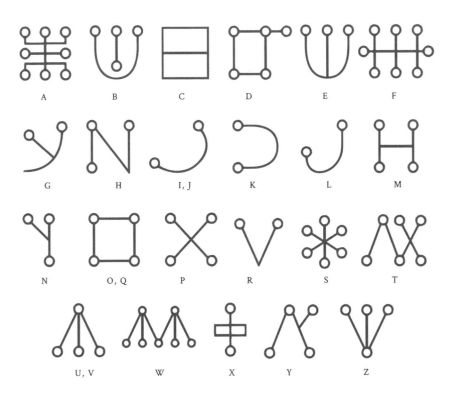

OGHAM ALPHABET

Inscriptions written in the Ogham alphabet have been found in Britain and Ireland dating from the 4th century CE. While all surviving examples of Ogham are inscriptions found on stone, it was probably more commonly inscribed on sticks, stakes and trees. One theory concerning its origin is that it was designed by the Irish so as not to be understood by those who read the Latin alphabet – that is, the authorities of Roman Britain. A second school of thought believes that Ogham was invented by the first Christian communities in early Ireland, out of a desire to have a unique alphabet for writing short messages and inscriptions in the Irish language – the sounds of primitive Irish being difficult to transcribe into Latin.

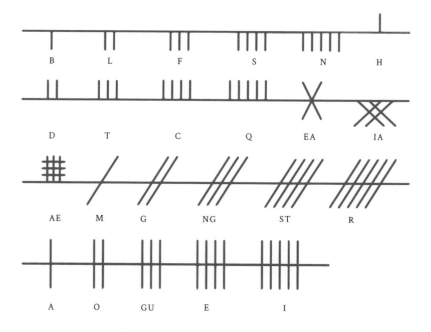

THEBAN ALPHABET

The Theban alphabet was first published in Johannes Trithemius's *Polygraphia* of 1518, in which it was attributed to Honorius of Thebes. It is also known as the Runes of Honorius, although Theban is not a runic alphabet. Another name is the witches' alphabet, due to its use in modern Wicca and witchcraft as a cipher to hide magical writings from the uninitiated.

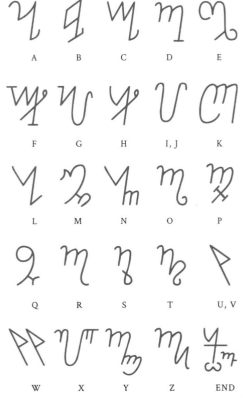

TIME, SHAPE, NUMBER AND COLOUR

Concepts of time, shape, number and colour enable us to communicate and create. Measuring time gives humans some feeling of control over their lives and the ability to make plans. Shapes carry archetypal meaning and symbolize aspects of our world, communicating meaning on their own and adding meaning to other complex symbols. In sacred geometry, the proportions, shapes or symmetries of a form have special significance, while from ancient times numbers have been seen as keys to the mysteries of the cosmos. Colour also is associated with different secular and religious meanings.

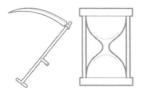

Time

The desire to measure time probably began with the realization that the sun rose in the east and disappeared in the west, only to reappear in the east the following morning. The earliest clock was probably the moon, which enabled hunter-gatherers to match the passing of the seasons with its phases. From this early time-keeper, more sophisticated methods of measuring time evolved.

SCYTHE

A curved blade mounted on a shaft, a scythe is used for mowing grasses. It may be held by the Greek god Chronus or the Roman god Saturn, both gods of time (the word 'chronology' stems from the Greek *khronos*, meaning 'time'). The scythe as an emblem of time cuts the thread of life and launches us one by one into eternity.

HOURGLASS

The hourglass represents the upper and lower worlds, the narrow opening showing the difficulty of transition between them. The hourglass stands for creation and destruction, life and death. The alchemical sign for hour was two semicircles on top of each other, as in the hourglass. In modern culture, the hourglass symbolizes the relentless passage of time, whether or not one notices its passage.

FATHER TIME

Father Time, who is usually depicted as an elderly bearded man carrying a scythe or hourglass, is a symbol of passing time. He is sometimes paired with Mother Nature as a married couple. Father Time is a more modern version of the Greek Chronus and Roman Saturn and the Hindu Shani. In New Year traditions, such as greetings cards, Father Time personifies the old year who hands over the duties of time to the baby in nappies who personifies the new year.

GRIM REAPER

In Western cultures, death is often personified as the Grim Reaper and depicted as a skeleton carrying a large scythe and wearing a black robe with a hood. In some tales, the Grim Reaper is said to actually cause the victim's death, leading to stories that he can be bribed or outwitted, thereby delaying the inevitable. In other stories he is a psychopomp, a spirit who severs the final tie of the soul to the body and guides the deceased to the next world. The character Death has appeared in many novels, plays and films over the centuries.

Shape

Shapes like the triangle, circle, square and spiral form the foundations of mystical symbolism. The dynamic shape of the circle is found everywhere in nature and represents the union of the earth and heaven. Unlike the circle, the square is a human-made form that symbolizes stability and the earth. The zigzag is a primal shape that has had numerous symbolic meanings, while the cross within a circle is believed to be one of the most ancient symbols in the world.

TRIANGLE

The triangle is a symbol of ethics as it suggests mathematical exactness and method applied to spiritual problems. The triangle is a symbol for truth, the key to science and wisdom. Its study leads to revelations of the mystery of life.

The equilateral triangle is associated with the divine number three that in Christian symbolism stands for the Holy Trinity. Philosophically, the triangle symbolizes the thesis giving rise to its antithesis, and these two together creating a synthesis. It is through the tension of opposites that something new is created.

The triangle is a symbol for power and as such relates to danger, but it also means safety and sometimes success and prosperity. For the ancient Hittites, the triangle was used to convey a meaning of well, good or healthy.

In the eastern Tantric tradition, one of the symbols used for representing the female principle is a triangle. This tantric triangle represents the vulva or yoni, or possibly the womb.

CIRCLE

The circle is a symbol found in all cultures throughout all ages and may have been the first shape drawn by humans. The circle symbolizes the sun – essential for life – as well as wholeness, completeness, illumination, the cycle of life, death and rebirth, the Wheel of Life, the Philosopher's Stone of alchemy and, in many religious traditions, the all-seeing or all-knowing eye. The circle has no beginning or end, so it is a universal symbol of eternity, perfection, divinity, infinity and the cosmos. This shape symbolizes time and the cycles of the natural world, the moon, the planets and the zodiac.

The circle also represents unity and is often used to signify and promote equality, as in the circular-shaped United Nations Assembly or the Round Table of King Arthur. For many cultures, the circle had magical functions symbolizing protection and the creation of a magical boundary that could not be crossed. In jewellery, the protective circle takes the form of a ring, bracelet, necklace, belt or crown.

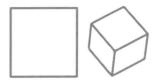

SQUARE

The square represents the earth and that which is created, as opposed to the circle, which represents heaven and uncreated, primordial energy. The square symbolizes the physical world and space because it can reside on both the horizontal and vertical planes. In Buddhism, the square forms the base of the stupa and represents the earth. This shape functions as the archetype of order in the universe and the standard of proportion – the square being equal on all sides and angles. The expression 'four-square' means one marked by firm, unwavering conviction, and promises stability and permanence.

To Pythagoras in the 6th century BCE, the square represented perfection. In Christian art, it refers to the Four Evangelists. Hindu or Buddhist mandalas that are images of the cosmos are often pictured as squares, with gates representing the four cardinal directions. In China, the earth was viewed as square and the square was an imperial emblem because the emperor was Lord of the Earth. The square signifies land, field, ground or the element earth. In modern meteorology, it represents the ground.

CUBE

The cube – a square in three dimensions, with each face identical to the others – represents truth as, no matter which way it is viewed, it remains the same. Because it cannot be rotated, it symbolizes stability. In Islam and Judaism, the cube represents the core of the faith. The Kaaba, the holiest shrine in Mecca, is constructed in the shape of a double cube. In early Kabbalist scriptures it is said that the angel Metatron created an elaborate talisman out of his own soul, which was based on the shape of a flattened cube. Considered a holy glyph, it was often drawn around an object or person to ward off demons and satanic powers.

LABYRINTH

As a shape, the labyrinth is a winding form that folds back on itself, with a single path leading to the centre and back. Labyrinths are represented symbolically as drawings or physically on the ground, where they can be walked from their entry points to the centre and back out again. They have historically been used in both group rituals and for private meditation. The labyrinth symbolizes a psychological or spiritual journey to the centre of one's psyche or soul, to experience insight and then return to the everyday world transformed.

SPIRAL

The spiral is common in the natural world, appearing in both the plant and animal kingdoms. Not surprisingly, the spiral is one of the most ancient symbols and features frequently in megalithic art, notably in the Newgrange passage tomb in Ireland. Its appearance at other burial sites around the world suggests that the spiral was a universal symbol for the cycle of life, death and rebirth. It may also have signified the sun, which appeared to die each night and be born again each morning. Ancient Chinese roof tiles were often decorated with the spiral. The spiral as a lunar, fertility symbol was often engraved upon Palaeolithic images of goddesses.

On a cosmic level, it represented the cyclical nature of life and the reality of the constant dynamic movement of all things.

In ancient Celtic symbolism, a loosely wound anticlockwise spiral represented the summer sun, while a tightly wound clockwise spiral symbolized the weaker winter sun. Double spirals signified the equinoxes. Spirals woven on carpets or cloth were believed to provide magical protective powers.

ZIGZAG

The zigzag is a primal shape that has had many symbolic meanings. The ancient Babylonians made use of it as a symbol of lightning. Their god of storms and wind, Adad, was depicted holding a zigzag in his hand. Neolithic bone fragments found in France dating back 300,000 years were also inscribed with zigzags, possibly symbolizing water or snakes.

In ancient Egyptian hieroglyphs a zigzag symbolized water and the zigzag is a symbol of the zodiac sign of Aquarius. The letter S in the Norse runic alphabet is in the shape of a zigzag or lightning flash. In modern times, a zigzag near electric installations indicates danger of electrocution. In Ghana the zigzag, known as *owo akoforo* adobe or 'snake climbs a palm tree', represents the exercise of wisdom, tactfulness and prudence. The zigzag symbol is carved on the President of Ghana's Chair of State. The zigzag is also found on African kente cloth designs.

CROSS

The solar cross, or cross within a circle, is probably one of the oldest symbols in the world. It represented the sun and the recurring cyclical nature of the seasons, and has appeared in Asian, American, European and Indian art from the dawn of history. After losing its rim, it appeared as a four-armed free-standing cross, which was used to show the shadows cast by the rising and setting sun at the summer and winter solstices. A six-armed cross depicted the sunrise and sunset shadows of the equinoxes.

As an archetypal shape or symbol, the four-armed cross also represents the world axis, *axis mundi*, or the great pole around which the different constellations of the zodiac revolve. As the mystic centre of the cosmos, the cross became a vehicle through which humans could access the divine realms. The cross is a combination of two different signs that symbolize the dual nature of human concerns, the marrying of the physical and the spiritual and of active and passive energies. The vertical axis (the upright pole or symbolic ladder) of the cross represents the spiritual impulse to reach the divine, while the horizontal crosspiece represents worldly or temporal concerns.

Sacred geometry

In sacred geometry, the proportions, shape or symmetry of a form create harmonious structures that are not only pleasing but also connect with the larger energies of the universe. The golden ratio is one example of sacred geometry, used by Leonardo da Vinci (1452–1519) and many others in paintings, sculpture, city planning and architecture. The Fibonacci sequence is another example that many plants and animals naturally embody as they grow.

GOLDEN RATIO

The golden ratio – which is also known as the divine proportion or golden mean – is represented mathematically as 1:1.618 and is often denoted by the Greek letter Phi. It appears in nature as well as in human-made designs. Mathematicians, such as Pythagoras and Euclid in ancient Greece, the medieval Italian Leonardo of Pisa, the Renaissance astronomer Johannes Kepler and present-day Oxford physicist Roger Penrose, have been fascinated by the golden ratio. Biologists, artists, musicians, historians, architects, psychologists and mystics have marvelled at the golden ratio's worldwide prevalence and appeal.

Since the Renaissance, many artists and architects from around the world have used this ratio in creating their works, because it was thought to be aesthetically pleasing. For example, the Greek sculptor Phidias (c.490–430 BCE) seems to have used the golden ratio in creating the statues at the Parthenon in Athens. The Great Mosque of Kairouan reveals the golden ratio throughout its design. And the shape of the Great Pyramid at Giza in Egypt is very close to the proportions of the golden ratio.

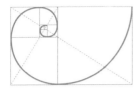

THE FIBONACCI SEQUENCE

Leonardo of Pisa (c.1170–1250), the Italian mathematician known as Fibonacci, discovered a unique sequence of numbers that came to be termed the Fibonacci sequence. The series begins with zero and one, and then the previous two numbers are added together to get the next number, thus: 0, 1, 2, 3, 5, 8, 13, 21, 34, 55, 89, 144, etc. In 1202, in his book *Liber Abaci* or *The Book of Calculations*, Fibonacci introduced the sequence to Western European mathematicians.

Previously the Indian grammarian Pingala had described the sequence in his book on prosody (the metrical structure of verse), written around 450–200 BCE. Prosody was important for ancient Indians, who placed emphasis on the purity of speech. The Indian mathematician Virahanka (6th century CE) and the Jain philosopher Hemachandra (1089–1172 CE) continued the work, showing how the sequence related to the rhythmic structure of verse.

The Fibonacci sequence can be seen in the development of many plants and animals, including the spiral of nautilus seashells, sunflowers, daisies and pine cones, which have a Fibonacci sequential number of growing points. Mathematically, the Fibonacci sequence is closely related to the golden ratio.

150

I II

Number

The great mathematician Pythagoras (c. 580–c.500 BCE) believed that numbers ruled the universe. For him, even numbers symbolized the feminine principle and cyclical movement, while odd numbers represented the male principle and fixed positions. Medieval scholars believed that numbers had a divine source and possessed mystical powers. Each of the numbers that follows has its own imagery and significance for different peoples across the world.

ONE

The number one symbolizes unity and the first, the best and the only. It also represents harmony and peace. One stands independently and cannot be divided. In Christian and in the other monotheistic religions, the number one represents the one God, indivisible. It also symbolizes the primordial beginning from which all things originate. The single standing stone, the erect phallus and the staff represent the primal creativity of the number one.

TWO

Two represents yin and yang, polarity and the realm of opposites. It is the first number that can be divided and thus represents division and difference. This number is symbolic of the duality of day and night, sun and moon, good and evil, as well as the two aspects of Christ – divine and human. Pairs of guardian figures double the sense of protection, as in the pairs of lions that are sometimes used to decorate the entrances to temples and palaces.

III IV V VI

Three

This number has a holy connotation in many cultures and represents variations on the trio of heaven (or God), the earth (or the cosmos) and humankind. In Christianity, the Father, Son and Holy Spirit make up the Holy Trinity. The Hindu trinity is composed of the deities Brahma, Vishnu and Shiva. Buddhists take refuge in the Three Jewels: Buddha, Dharma and Sangha.

Four

Four represents solidity, the earth and material things and is linked to the symbols of the cross and the square. This number represents the four cardinal directions – north, south, east and west; the four seasons – summer, autumn, winter and spring; the four elements – air, fire, water and earth. Alchemists honoured the Divine Quaternity as a fundamental aspect of the completion of the Greater Work. Pythagoras communicated the ineffable name of God to his followers using the number four or the 'geometric square'.

Five

Standing in the middle of the first nine numbers, five is the number representing the centre and harmony. In China, five is the number of the centre – the ideogram of *wu* (five) being composed of a cross and the centre symbolizing the five elements. Five is also thought to be the symbol of the human being, composed of two arms, two legs and the head and body. It also represents the phenomenal world of the five senses.

Six

Six symbolizes perfection as power, manifested in the form of six equilateral triangles within a circle. However, this number also incorporates within it the confrontation of two threes, with the potential of creating as much harm as good. In the Book of Revelation, six is the number of sin and it symbolizes the deification of the power of the state over God. St Clement of Alexandria noted that the world was created in six days and in the six directions of space, which are the four cardinal directions, plus the nadir and zenith.

VII VIII IX X

SEVEN

Seven is a magical number symbolizing the perfection of a complete cycle. Each of the four phases of the moon has seven days and 7 x 4 equals 28 days, or a complete moon cycle. The sum of the first seven digits $(1 + 2 + 3 + 4 + 5 + 6 + 7)$ also equals 28. Seven symbolizes a dynamic wholeness. There are seven main chakras (energy centres) in the body and in Islam there are seven heavens, seven hells and seven earths. There are also seven days in the Jewish Passover. On the seventh day, God rested after creating the world.

EIGHT

Eight stands for balance. In Buddhism the eight-spoked wheel represents the Eightfold Path to Enlightenment and there are eight petals on the lotus on which the Buddha sits. There are Eight Trigrams in the Taoist I Ching and Eight Immortals. Many baptismal fonts in Christian churches are octagonal, because eight represents regeneration and renewal. The eighth day following the seven days of creation stands for the resurrection and transfiguration of Christ and therefore of the human race. The eighth card of older Tarot decks is Justice, which is a symbol of the final weighing and of balance.

NINE

Nine symbolizes ritual, gestation and exertion in pursuit of completion. Demeter wandered for nine days in search of her daughter Persephone. A woman is pregnant for nine months. Nine is a symbol of fulfilment, a complete journey before returning full circle to the number one. Infinity may be expressed by repetitions of the number nine, such as 999,999,999... In Chinese mythology, nine is the number of the celestial spheres, and therefore there were nine steps up to the emperor's throne. The Aztec king Nezahualcoyotl built his nine-storey temple to match the nine heavens.

TEN

For Pythagoras, ten was the universal divine number, the perfect number that provides the basis for the decimal system that may have evolved because humans can count to ten using the fingers and thumbs of both hands. In China, ten is known as a multiple (5 x 2) that expresses duality and motion and so represents both death and life. The Maya regarded the tenth day as unlucky because it was the day of the death god. St Augustine saw the number ten as the perfect expression of the sum of seven and three. The Ten Commandments give three laws relating to the love of God and seven to the love of humans.

XI XII XIII

ELEVEN
If ten is a complete, perfect number, then the number eleven – which is one too many – stands for excess, extravagance or promiscuity. This number also suggests conflict and ambivalence. It could mean the start of a new cycle or the unbalancing, collapse or corruption of the number ten. The number eleven suggests an individual striking out alone, in a rebellious or even lawless way, outside and without relationship to the cosmic whole. In African esoteric traditions, eleven is related to women and fertility – women having eleven body openings and men only nine.

TWELVE
The number twelve symbolizes the cycles of the universe and its divisions in time and space. The dome of heaven is divided into twelve sections, resulting in the twelve signs of the zodiac. The Assyrians, Jews and other peoples divided the year into twelve months. The Chinese and others in central Asia introduced twelve-year cycles, which, when multiplied by five, equal sixty years, the point at which the solar and lunar cycles converge. In Christianity there are twelve apostles, and rose windows in cathedrals were often divided into twelve sections.

THIRTEEN
Since classical antiquity, the number thirteen has been deemed unlucky and a portent of bad things to come. The Kabbalah identifies thirteen evil spirits. The thirteenth chapter of the Book of Revelation describes the Antichrist and the Beast. The thirteen at the Last Supper – the twelve apostles plus Christ – preceded the coming betrayal by Judas Iscariot. Numerologists consider the number thirteen to operate generally outside the laws of the universe in an unharmonious, erratic and marginal way. The ancient Aztecs used the number thirteen to divide time and kept a thirteen-day week.

Colour

In ancient civilizations, colour held mystical power as a manifestation of light and the divine. It is widely acknowledged that colour influences our mood and stirs the emotions; colour can either attract or repel. Many cultures have devised systems of colour with religious or secular meaning. The colour of images of the divine in Hinduism and Buddhism, the use of colour in Islam and the tinctures of heraldry are just a few examples.

BLUE

Blue represents both the vast expanse of the sky above and the unfathomable depths of the sea below. As a colour, blue is thought to be spiritual, infinite, empty, spacious and eternal. This is the coolest, most detached, least substantive of all colours, and is said to dematerialize whatever it touches. For example, a wall painted light blue can seem to shimmer and disappear. Blue also represents transparency and the world of dreams. It is the colour of that which is surreal and not of this world. The Egyptians, who painted the scenes of the weighing of the souls with a light sky-blue background, considered it the colour of truth.

The blue colour of the Virgin Mary's robe suggests her detachment from worldly life. For Buddhists, blue represents transcendent wisdom and emptiness. Royal blue is the colour of Nut, the Egyptian goddess of the night, who represents wisdom. The Hindu gods Krishna and Vishnu are depicted with blue bodies to signify their divinity. And the colour blue symbolizes the desire for purity and what transcends worldly life.

RED

Whether red is bright or dark makes a difference concerning what it represents. Bright red is the colour of fire, blood, heat and power, and as such is a symbol of the life force. Throughout Asia, bright red is a lucky colour. Buddhists consider it the colour of activity and creativity. In Japan only children and women wear bright red. It is also the hue that appears on flags, stop signs and emergency buttons indicating danger. Later Christianity considered bright red the symbol of lust and licentiousness and it was not favoured; it was the colour that represented martyred saints. Bright red is the colour of romance, passion, youth, beauty and emotion – a red-faced person is one who is angry or embarrassed.

Dark red, on the other hand, is seen as the red of spiritual initiation, of forbidden esoteric knowledge, of the blood inside the womb, of fire inside the earth and of the mysteries of life. It is the colour of the soul and the heart.

GREEN

Green is the colour of nature, fertility, hope, renewal and rebirth. In the Christian tradition, it symbolizes the triumph of life over death. Green is the liturgical colour used during the celebration of the Epiphany and for the Sundays after Pentecost. It is a sacred colour in Islam, representing fertility and spiritual knowledge. Those who enter Paradise are said to wear green robes. In the West, green is the colour of springtime and the start of a new life cycle. On a deeper level, it represents the hidden knowledge of the natural world. In China, green is connected to thunder and the arousing of yang energy in the spring. It corresponds to the wood element and represents longevity, strength and hope. Modern marketing tests have concluded that green is the most neutral and tranquil of all colours.

Green also represents death and putrefaction. The greenish complexion of the sick contrasts with the life-giving promise of new and tender shoots of grass. In a rose window at Chartres Cathedral in France, Satan is depicted with green skin.

YELLOW

Yellow, representing the brilliant rays of the sun, is the hottest, most expansive and intense of all colours. The colour yellow symbolizes the gods, youth and energy. In China, yellow is considered the colour of fertile soil, as well as the imperial hue. In Buddhism, yellow is the colour of the earth element.

In other times and cultures the colour yellow had less positive meanings. In medieval Europe, yellow was associated with deception and the doors of traitors' homes were painted yellow. In Chinese theatre, actors would paint their faces yellow to signify their character's cruelty and deceit. In Greek mythology, the golden apple was a symbol of love because Gaia had given it to Hera and Zeus as a wedding present; yet a golden apple called the Apple of Discord was a symbol of jealousy and pride and a cause of the Trojan War. In Islam, golden yellow symbolized wise counsel, while pale yellow indicated treachery. Today, in the English language, yellow is associated with cowardice.

PURPLE

Purple became the colour of royalty in the ancient world because purple dye was obtained from a scarce species of mollusc, making it very valuable. The Greek word for purple is *porphura*, referring to the name of the shellfish that was the source of the dye. Dark shades of purple continue to indicate wealth, royalty, nobility and ceremony, whereas lighter shades are considered feminine and light-hearted. Purple also symbolizes spirituality, creativity, wisdom and mystery. In the Book of Revelation, the colour purple symbolizes both riches and the corruption of riches. In the Old Testament it also represented judges and judgment.

When it appears in nature – as in the flowers of the lavender, orchid, lilac and violet – purple is considered delicate and precious. It is the colour of mourning for widows in Thailand, and is used at later stages of mourning in the West. The Purple Heart is a medal given to US soldiers who have been wounded during warfare.

BLACK

Black is the absence of light and is a sign of mourning in Islam and the Christian West. Throughout the world the colour black is associated with evil, harm and negative forces. Black is the colour of night, adversity and mystery. However, in mystical traditions, because it contains all colours, black is considered the colour of the divine and the symbol of undivided oneness. In Islam, the veil of the sacred Kaaba at Mecca is black. In the Christian tradition, black is associated with penance.

WHITE

White can signify the absence of all colour or the sum of all colour. As such, it is simultaneously stillness, quiet and potential, as shown in the white light of dawn. In the Christian tradition, white represents purity and virginity and is the liturgical colour of Easter. White is the colour of grace and divine manifestation and white haloes are often shown around the heads of those who have known the divine. In Islam, white symbolizes purity and peace. However, Hindu widows wear white as a sign of their loss, because white is the colour of mourning in Hinduism.